Everyman's Poetry

Everyman, I will go with thee,
and be thy guide

TO BE
DISPOSED
BY
AUTHORITY

John Donne

Selected and edited by D. J. ENRIGHT

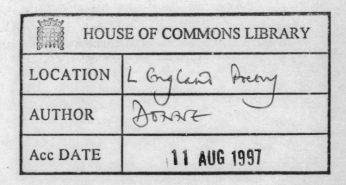

HOUSE OF COMMONS LIBRARY	
LOCATION	L England Poetry
AUTHOR	Donne
Acc DATE	11 AUG 1997

D0416150

Introduction and other critical apparatus
© J. M. Dent 1997

All rights reserved

J. M. Dent
Orion Publishing Group
Orion House
5 Upper St Martin's Lane
London WC2H 9EA

Typeset by Deltatype Ltd, Birkenhead, Merseyside

Printed in Great Britain by
The Guernsey Press Co. Ltd, Guernsey, C. I.

This book if bound as a paperback is subject to the condition
that it may not be issued on loan or otherwise except
in its original binding.

British Library Cataloguing-in-Publication
Data is available upon request.

ISBN 0 460 87901 4

Contents

Elegies

Epithalamions

Satires

Verse Letters

Divine Poems

Note on the Author and Editor

JOHN DONNE was born in 1572, the son of a prosperous London ironmonger; the family was Catholic, his mother related to Sir Thomas More (executed in 1535). Donne was enrolled at Hart Hall, Oxford, in 1584, and admitted to Lincoln's Inn as a law student in 1592. In London he was known as 'a great visitor of ladies, a great frequenter of plays'. In 1593 his younger brother Henry died of sickness in prison, having been arrested for sheltering a Catholic priest. At some point Donne abandoned the Catholic faith. He sailed under the Earl of Essex to sack Cadiz in 1596, and with the expedition to the Azores the following year. He was appointed secretary to Sir Thomas Egerton, the Lord Keeper (later Lord Chancellor), in 1598, but forfeited his worldly prospects when he secretly married Ann More, Lady Egerton's niece, in 1601; he was dismissed by Egerton and briefly imprisoned. The next twelve years or so were passed in poverty, without regular employment, although he acquired some loyal (if not very powerful) benefactors. James I urged him to enter the Church, and after some hesitation he did, in 1615. His wife died in 1617, at the age of 33, after giving birth to their twelfth child. In 1621 Donne was made Dean of St Paul's, and became a celebrated preacher. He died on 31 March 1631. The first collection of his poems was published in 1633.

D. J. ENRIGHT has taught and worked in publishing. Among his publications are books of criticism, memoirs and translations. His *Collected Poems* appeared in paperback in 1987 (Oxford University Press). He has edited *A Choice of Milton's Verse* (Faber, 1975), Johnson's *History of Rasselas* (Penguin, 1976) and, for Everyman Paperbacks, George Eliot's *Impressions of Theophrastus Such* (1995) and *George Herbert: Selected Poems* (1996); and also compiled several anthologies, including *The Oxford Book of Death* (Oxford University Press, 1983), *The Oxford Book of Friendship* (with David Rawlinson, 1991) and *The Oxford Book of the Supernatural* (1994).

Chronology of Donne's Life

Year	Age	Life
1572		Birth of Donne (sometime between 24 January and 19 June) in London, the third of six children of John and Elizabeth Donne, the latter a Catholic
1576	4	Death of father; mother marries Dr John Syminges
1577	5	Death of sister Elizabeth
1581	9	Death of sisters Mary and Katherine
1584	12	Matriculates at Hart Hall (now Hertford College), Oxford
1588	16	At Cambridge (?); death of stepfather
1589	17	Possibly abroad to 1591 (?)
1590	18	Mother marries Richard Rainsford (1591?)
1592	20	Admitted to Lincoln's Inn; Master of the Revels (1593)
1593	21	Death of brother Henry while held in Newgate Prison for sheltering a Catholic priest

Chronology of his Times

Year	Artistic Context	Historical Events
1572	Birth of Ben Jonson	Massacre of St Bartholomew
1575	Tasso, *Gerusalemme liberata*	
1577	Holinshed, *Chronicle*	Drake's circumnavigation of the globe begins
1579	Spenser, *Shepherd's Calendar* North, translation of Plutarch	
1580	Death of Camoëns Birth of John Webster (?) Montaigne, *Essais I–II*	
1584		William of Orange assassinated Ralegh's colonization of Virginia fails
1587	Marlowe, *Tamburlaine* (I–II) acted	Mary Queen of Scots executed
1588	Birth of Hobbes	Defeat of the Spanish Armada
1589	Marlowe, *Dr Faustus* first (?) acted	
1590	Spenser, *Faerie Queene* (I–III)	
1592	Death of Montaigne	
1593	Birth of George Herbert Birth of Izaak Walton Death of Marlowe	
1594	Death of Tintoretto	Swan Theatre built (1596?)

Year	Age	Life
1596	24	Takes part in expedition to Cadiz under Essex and Ralegh
1597	25	Takes part in expedition to the Azores
1598		Becomes secretary to Sir Thomas Egerton, the Lord Keeper
1601	29	Member of Parliament for Brackley, Northants; married secretly to Egerton's niece, Ann More
1602	30	Marriage made public; dismissed from Egerton's service and briefly imprisoned
1603	31	Daughter Constance born
1604	32	Son John born
1605	33	Travels to France and possibly Italy; third child George born
1606	34	Moves to Mitcham

Year	Artistic Context	Historical Events
1595	Sidney, *Apology for Poetry* Spenser, *Amoretti* and *Epithalamion* *A Midsummer Night's Dream* first (?) acted; also *Richard II*	War in Ulster Ralegh's voyage to Guiana
1596	Spenser, *Faerie Queene IV-VI* and *Four Hymns* *The Merchant of Venice* first (?) acted Birth of Descartes	The Edict of Nantes
1597	Bacon, first ten *Essays*	
1598		Death of Philip II of Spain
1599	Globe Theatre opened Death of Spenser *Julius Caesar* and *Henry V* first acted	Birth of Oliver Cromwell
1600	Birth of Calderón *Hamlet* first (?) acted William Gilbert, *De Magnete*	Birth of the future Charles I
1601	*Twelfth Night* first acted	Essex executed
1602	Bodleian Library, Oxford, opened	
1603		Death of Elizabeth I, succeeded by James I
1604	*Othello* first acted	Hampton Court Conference
1605	Bacon, *Advancement of Learning* Cervantes, *Don Quixote* Part I	The Gunpowder Plot Birth of Sir Thomas Browne
1606	*Macbeth*, *King Lear*, Jonson's *Volpone* and Tourneur's *Revenger's Tragedy* first (?) acted Birth of Rembrandt Birth of Corneille	

Year	Age	Life
1607	35	Takes lodgings in the Strand, London; fourth child Francis born
1608	36	Fifth child Lucy born; Countess of Bedford as godmother
1609	37	Sixth child Bridget born; 'The Expiration' published in Ferrabosco's *Airs*
1610	38	Obtains honorary MA from Oxford; *Pseudo-Martyr* published, dedicated to James I
1611	39	Seventh child Mary born; *Ignatius his Conclave* and *The First Anniversary* published; with Sir Robert Drury on the Continent (to 1612)
1612	40	Two *Anniversaries* published; also 'Break of Day' in Corkine's *Second Book of Airs*; eighth child stillborn
1613	41	Ninth child Nicholas born, died within the year; elegy on Prince Henry published in *Lachrymae lachrymarum* (3rd ed.)
1614	42	Member of Parliament for Taunton, Somerset; deaths of children Mary and Francis
1615	43	Ordained deacon and priest at St Paul's Cathedral; appointed a royal chaplain; made honorary DD at Cambridge; tenth child Margaret born
1616	44	Chosen Divinity Reader at Lincoln's Inn; eleventh child Elizabeth born

Year	Artistic Context	Historical Events
1607	*Antony and Cleopatra* first acted (1606?); also *Coriolanus* (1608?)	First successful English colony founded, in Virginia
1608	Birth of Milton	
1609	Shakespeare, *Sonnets*	
1610	Jonson, *Alchemist* first acted	Galileo reports on his telescopic view of the heavens Henri IV of France assassinated, succeeded by Louis XIII
1611	King James ('Authorized') Version of the Bible *The Winter's Tale* and *The Tempest* first acted Chapman's *Iliad* completed	Death of Charles IX of Sweden, succeeded by Gustavus Adolphus
1612		Death of heir apparent, Prince Henry Last burning of a heretic in England
1614	Ralegh, *History of the World* Webster, *Duchess of Malfi* first (?) acted Death of El Greco	
1616	Death of Shakespeare Jonson, *Works*	

Year	Age	Life
1617	45	Delivers first sermon at Paul's Cross, preaches widely thereafter; twelfth child stillborn (surviving by now: seven); death of wife Ann
1619	47	With Earl of Doncaster's embassy to Germany (to January 1620)
1621	49	Appointed Dean of St Paul's
1622	50	Two sermons published, followed by others (1623 ff.)
1623	51	Seriously ill
1624	52	*Devotions upon Emergent Occasions* published; appointed vicar of St Dunstan's
1627	55	Death of daughter Lucy; deaths of Lucy Countess of Bedford (patroness and friend) and Lady Magdalen Danvers (formerly Herbert)
1630	58	Final illness begins

Year	Artistic Context	Historical Events
1618	Birth of Cowley	The Thirty Years War Ralegh executed
1619	Inigo Jones begins the Whitehall Banqueting House (completed 1622)	
1620	Bacon, *Novum organum*	Pilgrim Fathers sail in the *Mayflower* and found Plymouth Colony in New England
1621	Burton, *Anatomy of Melancholy* Birth of Marvell, Vaughan and La Fontaine	Death of Philip III of Spain, succeeded by Philip IV
1622	Birth of Molière	
1623	First Shakespeare Folio Birth of Pascal	
1624		Cardinal Richelieu chief minister in France
1625	Death of Webster	Death of James I, succeeded by Charles I Outbreak of the Plague
1626	Death of Bacon Birth of John Aubrey	
1627		War with France (to 1629)
1628	William Harvey's treatise on the circulation of the blood published Birth of Bunyan	The Petition of Right Buckingham assassinated
1630		Birth of the future Charles II The Great Migration to Massachusetts begins; Boston founded

Year	Age	Life
1631	59	Dies 31 March, survived by six of his twelve children; buried in St Paul's
1633		*Poems, by J.D. with Elegies on the Author's Death* published

Year	Artistic Context	Historical Events
1631	Birth of Dryden	
1633	Death of George Herbert	

Introduction

In Thomas Mann's novel, *The Magic Mountain*, the young Hans Castorp, under the sway of the mysterious Clavdia Chauchat, expatiates on the kinship between *l'amour* and *la mort*, their shared terror and great magic. John Donne is our great poet of love, and of death. More mundanely, his work can be divided into three groups: the love poems; the occasional pieces, verse letters and satires; and the religious poetry. However widely the subjects differ, notably as between the love poems and the divine verse, the profane and the sacred, the poet's voice and his strategy are unmistakably the same.

The love poems embrace, separately or simultaneously, frank carnality, ecstatic spirituality, cynicism and bitterness, enthusiastic fulfilment, affirmations of constancy, torments of inconstancy, mischief and flippancy, forthright honesty, calculated disingenuousness – and bursts of grandeur, as witness 'She's all states, and all princes, I,/Nothing else is' ('The Sun Rising'). In an essay of 1933, 'On Metaphysical Poetry', James Smith proposed that Donne doesn't write about many things: 'He is content with the identity of lovers as lovers, and their diversity as the human beings in which love manifests itself; the stability and self-sufficiency of love, contrasted with the mutability and dependence of human beings; with the presence of lovers to each other, their physical unity, though they are separated by travel, and by death; the spirit demanding the succour of the flesh, the flesh hampering the spirit; the shortcomings of this life, summarized by decay and death, contrasted with the divine to which it aspires.' The 'things' may be limited, in both the love poems and the divine, but such are Donne's diversity of approach, his range of reference and his unflagging vigour, that the reader who doesn't stop to categorize is unlikely to be struck by any damaging repetitiousness.

While suggesting that Donne is truly metaphysical in the usual sense of the word, Smith notes that he customarily cites metaphysical propositions not as themselves necessarily true, 'but as possibly useful for inducing a belief in something else, which he believes is true'. It was Samuel Johnson who first applied the term 'metaphysical' to Donne and his followers, but in a figurative and predominantly unfavourable sense. Defining their brand of wit as 'a kind of *discordia concors*, a combination of dissimilar images, or discovery of occult resemblances in things apparently unlike', Johnson reckoned they had more than enough of it. 'The most heterogeneous ideas are yoked by violence together; nature and art are ransacked for illustrations, comparisons, and allusions; their learning instructs, and their subtlety surprises; but the reader commonly thinks his improvement dearly bought, and, though he sometimes admires, is seldom pleased.' These strictures apply to some of the verse of some of the poets Johnson was discussing; and it is easy to see how their 'unnaturalness' and lack of decorum in both matter and manner should offend the great Augustan. But in Donne, where passion and reason are in step, heterogeneous ideas flow one into another so persuasively that the result affects us as achieved naturally rather than enforced by violence. Even Johnson admitted that if the 'conceits' of the metaphysicals, their strange images and ingenious similitudes, were far-fetched, 'they were often worth the carriage', and that 'to write on their plan, it was at least necessary to read and think'.

In the spirit of the gentleman about town rather than the stern arbiter, Dryden declared that Donne 'affects the metaphysics not only in his satires but in his amorous verses, where nature only should reign, and perplexes the minds of the fair sex with nice speculations of philosophy, when he should engage their hearts, and entertain them with the softnesses of love'. Donne can be misogynous (he can be lots of things), but his demands on their minds imply a more substantial tribute to the fair sex than Dryden's patronizing advice to aim straight for their hearts. Though Donne's reputation lapsed badly in the eighteenth century and later, in the nineteenth he found a stout and perceptive champion in Coleridge, who advanced a different definition of wit as present in him: 'wonder-exciting vigour, intenseness and peculiarity of thought, using at will the almost boundless stores of a capacious memory, and exercised on subjects where we have no right to expect it'. (In its own idiom, Thomas Carew's elegy on Donne's death, published in 1633, has passages concerning the divine poems which are not unalike: 'a mine of rich and pregnant fancy', 'the flame/Of thy bright soul, that shot such heat and light . . ./Committed holy rapes upon our will' – lines that would invite the eighteenth century's charges of hyperbole and indelicacy!) And regarding Donne's supposed failure to respect metre, let alone attain any sustained musicality, Coleridge spoke the definitive word: 'in poems where the writer *thinks*, and expects the reader to do so, the sense must be understood in order to ascertain the metre'. To which one can only add that in practice arriving at the sense and recognizing the movement of the verse – rhythm rather than set metre – probably go together, each furthering the other.

'She's all states, and all princes, I,/Nothing else is.' The sun is old and needs rest, and since its job is to warm the world, it can do that in comfort by warming the two of them. Humour accompanies what without it wouldn't be grand so much as preposterous. And humour is a pervasive ingredient in Donne's speculative, fierce and intellectually unremitting habit of mind. We meet it in the conjecture that if the bickering philosophers had been more intelligent they would have seen that the beloved's fever could be the ultimate, universal conflagration. If 'audacious' isn't the word that comes to mind, not to say 'impudent', it is because of the calm, smiling and confidently reasonable tone in which the thought is couched. To adapt James Smith's remark, Donne knows these philosophers and their conflicting theories, and he invokes them to induce a belief in something quite different – the loved one's momentous significance for him. Humour often stems from the juxtaposition of contraries or incompatibles. The gallant's ungallant gibe in 'The Relic', 'For graves have learn'd that woman-head/ To be to more than one a bed' is succeeded only two lines later by the beautiful and resonant 'bracelet of bright hair about the bone', and then the suggestion, homely, amusing, and moving, that the purpose of the bracelet might be to ensure that at the Resurrection the lovers' souls 'meet at this grave, and make a little stay'. And 'To his Mistress Going to Bed', after all its equivocal grandiloquence ('O my America! my new-found-land'), isn't above concluding with a juvenile innuendo: 'What needst thou have more covering than a man?' Ribald humour can find a place in lovers' discourse; another poem asserts that 'Love's not so pure, and abstract, as they use/To say, which have no mistress but their Muse'.

King James, a patron of Donne's if only by making it plain that the sole advancement the poet would find was in the Church, is reported to have said that 'Dr Donne's verses were like the peace of

God, they passed all understanding'. (No doubt the more elevated the patron, the greater his need to assert superiority.) That Donne's poems pose problems today is undeniable, and unsurprising. (Hence the notes in the present book; and alas, once annotation has begun, there is no certain end to it.) Yet these difficulties are of no great force once the reader has grown accustomed to the character-istic manner, the thrust and flow of the speaking voice, the conspicuous element of drama, as present for example in the enactive line, 'Assail'd, fight, taken, stabb'd, bleed, fall, and die' ('Elegy 16'); and 'Batter my heart, three-person'd God; for, you/As yet but knock, breathe, shine, and seek to mend' ('Holy Sonnets: 14'), echoed in the wished-for opposites, 'break, blow, burn, and make me new'; and the famously strenuous passage in 'Satire 3': 'On a huge hill,/Cragged, and steep, Truth stands, and he that will/ Reach her, about must, and about must go'. We come to expect the unexpected (yet are still startled by it), and are prepared for the imagery, not so hard to master, drawn from cosmology, alchemy, philosophy, astronomy, geometry and medicine, from the 'new learning' of Copernicus and Paracelsus as well as the old learning of Ptolemy and Hippocrates, from religious disputes and voyages of discovery, from ancient mythology and contemporary affairs. (In an essay in *The Pelican Guide to English Literature*, Volume 3, 1956, R.G. Cox quoted these vivid and timeless lines on the London scene: 'As in our streets sly beggars narrowly/Watch motions of the giver's hand and eye,/And evermore conceive some hope thereby.')

It is true that we need to distinguish between the difficulty of what is difficult or puzzling by its very nature and the arduousness of ploughing through laboured analogies and strained logic. An instance of the latter is the fourth stanza of 'Epithalamion made at Lincoln's Inn', where a temple is in rapid succession a bosom, a womb, and a tomb. And that in 'To Sir Henry Wotton' Fate should feel such hate for some men as to marshal their state, or condemn them to pursue a career, at Court, perhaps owes less to reason than to rhyme. Such faults, infrequent in Donne, happen when sophistry prevails in the absence of conviction, and the poet is motivated more by duty than by zest. For the greater part F.R. Leavis's observation, in *Revaluation* (1936), is to the point: 'It is not any eccentricity or defiant audacity that makes the effect so immediate, but rather an irresistible rightness.'

Leavis had just quoted the opening stanza of 'The Good-Morrow':

> I wonder by my troth, what thou and I
> Did, till we lov'd? were we not wean'd till then?
> But suck'd on country pleasures, childishly?
> Or snorted we in the seven sleepers' den?
> 'Twas so; but this, all pleasures fancies be.
> If ever any beauty I did see,
> Which I desir'd, and got, 'twas but a dream of thee.

We take note of the pause after 'what thou and I', at the end of the line, and the subsequent stress laid on 'Did'. The light-hearted question, 'were we not wean'd till then?', has a more inventive and urbanely scornful sequel in 'But suck'd on country pleasures, childishly?', reinforced by the robust, comical verb, 'snorted', and the barely credible old story of the seven sleepers. Then comes the brief, dogmatic answer: ' 'Twas so', and, apropos of 'beauty', the expressively punctuated 'Which I desir'd, and got'. We see Donne today as an 'original', and he was original in his time, his verse at odds with the smoothness and irreproachable harmonies of the average Elizabethan lyric. As Leavis claimed, the reader, coming across the poem in an anthology of the period, would cease reading as a student and read on 'as we read the living'.

What Donne said of Mr Tilman 'after he had taken orders' might be said, with some reservations, of the author of the divine poems: 'Thou art the same materials, as before,/Only the stamp is changed; but no more'. Another kind of love is at issue, it is true, other manifestations of doubt, fear, despair, intimacy, hope, inconstancy or perverse constancy ('Inconstancy unnaturally hath begot/A constant habit'), and – in 'A Hymn to God the Father', one of the last poems Donne wrote and perhaps the finest – entreaty: 'Wilt thou forgive that sin . . . ?', modulating into a provisional assurance: 'having done that, thou hast done,/I fear no more'. The compelling power of the speaking voice – Donne was a powerful preacher – is at work everywhere in the divine poems too: in the desolation of 'Despair behind, and death before doth cast/Such terror'; the triumphant, urbanely condescending declaration, 'For, those, whom thou think'st thou dost overthrow,/Die not, poor death'; and the glory of 'arise, arise/From death, you numberless infinities/Of souls, and to your scatter'd bodies go'. Here too is the 'mimetic flexibility' that Leavis identified in 'Satire 3', the right words in the right rhythm.

Carew ended his elegy or eulogy on Donne by glancing at the two aspects of the man and the poet: 'Here lie two flamens, and both those, the best,/Apollo's first, at last, the true God's priest'. George Herbert, another 'original' and rival for the title of our supreme Christian poet, was never a priest of Apollo, much less of Cupid. But both poets argue in their verse, with themselves and with God. In his *Devotions upon Emergent Occasions* Donne said, 'I have not the righteousness of Job, but I have the desire of Job: I would speak to the Almighty, and I would reason with God.' God is to be feared and revered, but a man's a man for all that.

Note on the Text

Very few of Donne's poems were printed during his lifetime, but there are numerous manuscripts, in various hands and with variable readings, which circulated among his friends. The first printed collection appeared posthumously in 1633, with further editions in 1635 and onwards. The present text is largely based on the collection of 1633 (preferred by Herbert J. Grierson, whose pioneering edition came out in 1912), but incorporates variants from the manuscripts when these seem superior.

Spelling has been modernized; and likewise punctuation – up to a point, since the original punctuation quite often creates a vivid effect, for instance an emphasizing pause, characteristic of the speaking voice. I have also reduced a plethora of capital letters to lower case.

Words such as 'joined' and 'cursed', spelt thus, are to be pronounced as two syllables, 'restored' and 'published' as three, and so forth. When the *e* is elided, the word is pronounced as one syllable, e.g. 'lov'd' and 'turn'd', or as two syllables, e.g. 'worshipp'd', 'compar'd', etc. Similarly 'th'earth' is monosyllabic, 'th'other' disyllabic, etc. Other special pronunciations are indicated in the notes.

John Donne

Songs and Sonnets

The Good-Morrow

I wonder by my troth, what thou and I
Did, till we lov'd? were we not wean'd till then?
But suck'd on country pleasures, childishly?
Or snorted we in the seven sleepers' den?
'Twas so; but this, all pleasures fancies be.   5
If ever any beauty I did see,
Which I desir'd, and got, 'twas but a dream of thee.

And now good-morrow to our waking souls,
Which watch not one another out of fear;
For love all love of other sights controls,   10
And makes one little room an everywhere.
Let sea-discoverers to new worlds have gone,
Let maps to other, worlds on worlds have shown,
Let us possess one world, each hath one, and is one.

My face in thine eye, thine in mine appears,   15
And true plain hearts do in the faces rest;
Where can we find two better hemispheres
Without sharp north, without declining west?
What ever dies, was not mixt equally;
If our two loves be one, or thou and I   20
Love so alike that none do slacken, none can die.

Song

Go, and catch a falling star,
 Get with child a mandrake root,
Tell me, where all past years are,
 Or who cleft the Devil's foot,
Teach me to hear mermaids singing,   5
Or to keep off envy's stinging,
    And find
    What wind
Serves to advance an honest mind.

If thou be'st born to strange sights,   10
 Things invisible to see,
Ride ten thousand days and nights,
 Till age snow white hairs on thee,
Thou, when thou return'st, wilt tell me
All strange wonders that befell thee,   15
    And swear
    No where
Lives a woman true, and fair.

If thou find'st one, let me know,
 Such a pilgrimage were sweet;   20
Yet do not, I would not go,
 Though at next door we might meet,
Though she were true, when you met her,
And last, till you write your letter,
    Yet she   25
    Will be
False, ere I come, to two, or three.

Woman's Constancy

Now thou hast lov'd me one whole day,
Tomorrow when thou leav'st, what wilt thou say?
Wilt thou then antedate some new made vow?
        Or say that now
We are not just those persons, which we were?   5
Or, that oaths made in reverential fear
Of Love, and his wrath, any may forswear?
Or, as true deaths true marriages untie,
So lovers' contracts, images of those,
Bind but till sleep, death's image, them unloose?   10
        Or, your own end to justify,
For having purpos'd change, and falsehood, you
Can have no way but falsehood to be true?
Vain lunatic, against these 'scapes I could
        Dispute, and conquer, if I would,   15
        Which I abstain to do,
For by tomorrow, I may think so too.

The Undertaking

I have done one braver thing
　　Than all the Worthies did,
And yet a braver thence doth spring,
　　Which is, to keep that hid.

It were but madness now t'impart　　　　5
　　The skill of specular stone,
When he which can have learn'd the art
　　To cut it, can find none.

So, if I now should utter this,
　　Others (because no more　　　　　10
Such stuff to work upon, there is)
　　Would love but as before.

But he who loveliness within
　　Hath found, all outward loathes,
For he who colour loves, and skin,　　　15
　　Loves but their oldest clothes.

If, as I have, you also do
　　Virtue attir'd in woman see,
And dare love that, and say so too,
　　And forget the He and She;　　　　20

And if this love, though placed so,
　　From profane men you hide,
Which will no faith on this bestow,
　　Or, if they do, deride:

Then you have done a braver thing　　　25
　　Than all the Worthies did;
And a braver thence will spring,
　　Which is, to keep that hid.

The Sun Rising

Busy old fool, unruly sun,
    Why dost thou thus,
Through windows, and through curtains call on us?
Must to thy motions lovers' seasons run?
    Saucy, pedantic wretch, go chide   5
    Late schoolboys, and sour prentices,
  Go tell court-huntsmen, that the King will ride,
  Call country ants to harvest offices;
Love, all alike, no season knows, nor clime,
Nor hours, days, months, which are the rags of time.   10

Thy beams so reverend, and strong
    Why shouldst thou think?
I could eclipse and cloud them with a wink,
But that I would not lose her sight so long:
    If her eyes have not blinded thine,   15
    Look, and tomorrow late, tell me,
  Whether both th' Indias of spice and mine
  Be where thou left'st them, or lie here with me.
Ask for those kings whom thou saw'st yesterday,
And thou shalt hear, All here in one bed lay.   20

She's all states, and all princes, I,
    Nothing else is.
Princes do but play us; compar'd to this,
All honour's mimic; all wealth alchemy.
    Thou sun art half as happy as we,   25
    In that the world's contracted thus;
  Thine age asks ease, and since thy duties be
  To warm the world, that's done in warming us.
Shine here to us, and thou art everywhere;
This bed thy centre is, these walls, thy sphere.   30

The Canonization

For God's sake hold your tongue, and let me love;
  Or chide my palsy, or my gout,
My five grey hairs, or ruin'd fortune flout;
    With wealth your state, your mind with arts improve,
      Take you a course, get you a place,   5
      Observe his Honour, or his Grace,
Or the King's real, or his stamp'd face
    Contemplate; what you will, approve,
    So you will let me love.

Alas, alas, who's injur'd by my love?   10
  What merchant's ships have my sighs drown'd?
Who says my tears have overflow'd his ground?
    When did my colds a forward spring remove?
      When did the heats which my veins fill
      Add one more to the plaguy bill?   15
Soldiers find wars, and lawyers find out still
    Litigious men, which quarrels move,
    Though she and I do love.

Call us what you will, we are made such by love;
  Call her one, me another fly,   20
We're tapers too, and at our own cost die,
    And we in us find the eagle and the dove.
      The phœnix riddle hath more wit
      By us; we two being one, are it.
So, to one neutral thing both sexes fit.   25
    We die and rise the same, and prove
    Mysterious by this love.

We can die by it, if not live by love,
  And if unfit for tombs and hearse
Our legend be, it will be fit for verse;   30
    And if no piece of chronicle we prove,
      We'll build in sonnets pretty rooms;

As well a well-wrought urn becomes
The greatest ashes, as half-acre tombs,
   And by these hymns, all shall approve   35
   Us canonized for love:

And thus invoke us: You whom reverend love
   Made one another's hermitage;
You, to whom love was peace, that now is rage;
   Who did the whole world's soul contract, and drove   40
      Into the glasses of your eyes,
      So made such mirrors, and such spies,
That they did all to you epitomize
   Countries, towns, courts: beg from above
   A pattern of your love!   45

The Triple Fool

I am two fools, I know,
For loving, and for saying so
   In whining poetry;
But where's that wise man, that would not be I,
   If she would not deny?   5
Then as th' earth's inward narrow crooked lanes
Do purge sea-water's fretful salt away,
   I thought, if I could draw my pains
Through rhyme's vexation, I should them allay.
Grief brought to numbers cannot be so fierce,   10
For he tames it, that fetters it in verse.

   But when I have done so,
Some man, his art and voice to show,
   Doth set and sing my pain,
And, by delighting many, frees again   15
   Grief, which verse did restrain.
To love and grief tribute of verse belongs,
But not of such as pleases when 'tis read;
   Both are increased by such songs:
For both their triumphs so are published,   20
And I, which was two fools, do so grow three;
Who are a little wise, the best fools be.

Lovers' Infiniteness

If yet I have not all thy love,
Dear, I shall never have it all;
I cannot breathe one other sigh, to move,
Nor can entreat one other tear to fall,
And all my treasure, which should purchase thee,   5
Sighs, tears, and oaths, and letters I have spent.
Yet no more can be due to me,
Than at the bargain made was meant.
If then thy gift of love were partial,
That some to me, some should to others fall,   10
    Dear, I shall never have thee all.

Or if then thou gavest me all,
All was but all, which thou hadst then;
But if in thy heart, since, there be or shall
New love created be, by other men,   15
Which have their stocks entire, and can in tears,
In sighs, in oaths, and letters outbid me,
This new love may beget new fears,
For, this love was not vow'd by thee.
And yet it was, thy gift being general,   20
The ground, thy heart, is mine; whatever shall
    Grow there, dear, I should have it all.

Yet I would not have all yet,
He that hath all can have no more,
And since my love doth every day admit   25
New growth, thou shouldst have new rewards in store;
Thou canst not every day give me thy heart,
If thou canst give it, then thou never gavest it:
Love's riddles are, that though thy heart depart,
It stays at home, and thou with losing savest it: 30
But we will have a way more liberal,
Than changing hearts, to join them, so we shall
    Be one, and one another's all.

Song

Sweetest love, I do not go,
  For weariness of thee,
Nor in hope the world can show
  A fitter love for me;
    But since that I   5
Must die at last, 'tis best,
To use my self in jest
  Thus by feign'd deaths to die.

Yesternight the sun went hence,
  And yet is here today;   10
He hath no desire nor sense,
  Nor half so short a way:
    Then fear not me,
But believe that I shall make
Speedier journeys, since I take   15
  More wings and spurs than he.

O how feeble is man's power,
  That if good fortune fall,
Cannot add another hour,
  Nor a lost hour recall!   20
    But come bad chance,
And we join to it our strength,
And we teach it art and length,
  Itself o'er us to advance.

When thou sigh'st, thou sigh'st not wind,   25
  But sigh'st my soul away,
When thou weep'st, unkindly kind,
  My life's blood doth decay.
    It cannot be
That thou lov'st me, as thou say'st,   30
If in thine my life thou waste,
  Thou art the best of me.

Let not thy divining heart
  Forethink me any ill,
Destiny may take thy part,   35
  And may thy fears fulfil;
    But think that we
Are but turn'd aside to sleep;
They who one another keep
  Alive, ne'er parted be.   40

A Fever

Oh do not die, for I shall hate
   All women so, when thou art gone,
That thee I shall not celebrate,
   When I remember, thou wast one.

But yet thou canst not die, I know;   5
   To leave this world behind, is death,
But when thou from this world wilt go,
   The whole world vapours with thy breath.

Or if, when thou, the world's soul, goest,
   It stay, 'tis but thy carcass then,   10
The fairest woman, but thy ghost,
   But corrupt worms, the worthiest men.

O wrangling schools, that search what fire
   Shall burn this world, had none the wit
Unto this knowledge to aspire,   15
   That this her fever might be it?

And yet she cannot waste by this,
   Nor long bear this torturing wrong,
For much corruption needful is
   To fuel such a fever long.   20

These burning fits but meteors be,
   Whose matter in thee is soon spent.
Thy beauty, and all parts, which are thee,
   Are unchangeable firmament.

Yet 'twas of my mind, seizing thee,   25
   Though it in thee cannot persever.
For I had rather owner be
   Of thee one hour, than all else ever.

Air and Angels

Twice or thrice had I loved thee,
Before I knew thy face or name;
So in a voice, so in a shapeless flame,
Angels affect us oft, and worshipp'd be;
    Still when, to where thou wert, I came, 5
Some lovely glorious nothing I did see.
    But since my soul, whose child love is,
Takes limbs of flesh, and else could nothing do,
    More subtle than the parent is
Love must not be, but take a body too, 10
    And therefore what thou wert, and who,
        I bid love ask, and now
That it assume thy body, I allow,
And fix itself in thy lip, eye, and brow.

Whilst thus to ballast love, I thought, 15
And so more steadily to have gone,
With wares which would sink admiration,
I saw, I had love's pinnace overfraught;
    Every thy hair for love to work upon
Is much too much, some fitter must be sought; 20
    For, nor in nothing, nor in things
Extreme, and scatt'ring bright, can love inhere;
    Then as an angel, face and wings
Of air, not pure as it, yet pure doth wear,
    So thy love may be my love's sphere; 25
        Just such disparity
As is 'twixt air and angels' purity,
'Twixt women's love, and men's will ever be.

The Anniversary

All kings, and all their favourites,
   All glory of honours, beauties, wits,
The sun itself, which makes times, as they pass,
Is elder by a year, now, than it was
When thou and I first one another saw: 5
All other things to their destruction draw,
   Only our love hath no decay;
This, no tomorrow hath, nor yesterday,
Running it never runs from us away,
But truly keeps his first, last, everlasting day.   10

Two graves must hide thine and my corse,
   If one might, death were no divorce.
Alas, as well as other princes, we
(Who prince enough in one another be)
Must leave at last in death, these eyes, and ears,   15
Oft fed with true oaths, and with sweet salt tears;
   But souls where nothing dwells but love
(All other thoughts being inmates) then shall prove
This, or a love increased there above,
When bodies to their graves, souls from their graves remove.   20

And then we shall be throughly blest,
   But we no more, than all the rest;
Here upon earth, we're kings, and none but we
Can be such kings, nor of such subjects be.
Who is so safe as we? where none can do   25
Treason to us, except one of us two.
   True and false fears let us refrain,
Let us love nobly, and live, and add again
Years and years unto years, till we attain
To write threescore: this is the second of our reign.   30

Twickenham Garden

Blasted with sighs, and surrounded with tears,
   Hither I come to seek the spring,
   And at mine eyes, and at mine ears,
Receive such balms, as else cure everything;
   But O, self-traitor, I do bring   5
The spider love, which transubstantiates all,
   And can convert manna to gall,
And that this place may thoroughly be thought
   True paradise, I have the serpent brought.

'Twere wholesomer for me, that winter did   10
   Benight the glory of this place,
   And that a grave frost did forbid
These trees to laugh, and mock me to my face;
   But that I may not this disgrace
Endure, nor yet leave loving, Love, let me   15
   Some senseless piece of this place be;
Make me a mandrake, so I may groan here,
   Or a stone fountain weeping out my year.

Hither with crystal vials, lovers come,
   And take my tears, which are love's wine,   20
   And try your mistress' tears at home,
For all are false, that taste not just like mine;
   Alas, hearts do not in eyes shine,
Nor can you more judge woman's thoughts by tears,
   Than by her shadow, what she wears.   25
O perverse sex, where none is true but she,
   Who's therefore true, because her truth kills me.

Love's Growth

I scarce believe my love to be so pure
    As I had thought it was,
    Because it doth endure
Vicissitude, and season, as the grass;
Methinks I lied all winter, when I swore,   5
My love was infinite, if spring make it more.
But if this medicine, love, which cures all sorrow
With more, not only be no quintessence,
But mixt of all stuffs, paining soul, or sense,
And of the sun his working vigour borrow,   10
Love's not so pure, and abstract, as they use
To say, which have no mistress but their Muse,
But as all else, being elemented too,
Love sometimes would contemplate, sometimes do.

And yet no greater, but more eminent,   15
    Love by the spring is grown;
    As, in the firmament,
Stars by the sun are not enlarg'd, but shown,
Gentle love deeds, as blossoms on a bough,
From love's awakened root do bud out now.   20
If, as in water stirr'd more circles be
Produc'd by one, love such additions take,
Those like so many spheres, but one heaven make,
For, they are all concentric unto thee.
And though each spring do add to love new heat,   25
As princes do in times of action get
New taxes, and remit them not in peace,
No winter shall abate the spring's increase.

The Dream

Dear love, for nothing less than thee
Would I have broke this happy dream,
   It was a theme
For reason, much too strong for fantasy,
Therefore thou waked'st me wisely; yet   5
My dream thou brok'st not, but continued'st it;
Thou art so truth, that thoughts of thee suffice,
To make dreams truths, and fables histories;
Enter these arms, for since thou thought'st it best,
Not to dream all my dream, let's act the rest.   10

As lightning, or a taper's light,
Thine eyes, and not thy noise wak'd me;
   Yet I thought thee
(For thou lovest truth) an angel, at first sight,
But when I saw thou saw'st my heart,   15
And knew'st my thoughts, beyond an angel's art,
When thou knew'st what I dreamt, when thou knew'st when
Excess of joy would wake me, and cam'st then,
I must confess, it could not choose but be
Profane, to think thee anything but thee.   20

Coming and staying show'd thee, thee,
But rising makes me doubt, that now,
   Thou art not thou.
That love is weak, where fear's as strong as he;
'Tis not all spirit, pure, and brave,   25
If mixture it of fear, shame, honour, have.
Perchance as torches which must ready be,
Men light and put out, so thou deal'st with me,
Thou cam'st to kindle, goest to come; then I
Will dream that hope again, but else would die.   30

A Valediction: Of Weeping

    Let me pour forth
My tears before thy face, whilst I stay here,
For thy face coins them, and thy stamp they bear,
And by this mintage they are something worth,
        For thus they be   5
        Pregnant of thee;
Fruits of much grief they are, emblems of more;
When a tear falls, that thou falls which it bore,
So thou and I are nothing then, when on a diverse shore.

    On a round ball   10
A workman that hath copies by, can lay
An Europe, Afric, and an Asia,
And quickly make that, which was nothing, all,
        So doth each tear,
        Which thee doth wear,   15
A globe, yea world by that impression grow,
Till thy tears mixt with mine do overflow
This world, by waters sent from thee, my heaven dissolved so.

    O more than moon,
Draw not up seas to drown me in thy sphere,   20
Weep me not dead, in thine arms, but forbear
To teach the sea, what it may do too soon;
        Let not the wind
        Example find,
To do me more harm, than it purposeth;   25
Since thou and I sigh one another's breath,
Whoe'er sighs most, is cruellest, and hastes the other's death.

Love's Alchemy

Some that have deeper digg'd love's mine than I,
Say, where his centric happiness doth lie.
      I have lov'd, and got, and told,
But should I love, get, tell, till I were old,
I should not find that hidden mystery;   5
        Oh, 'tis imposture all:
And as no chemic yet th'elixir got,
        But glorifies his pregnant pot,
        If by the way to him befall
Some odoriferous thing, or medicinal,   10
   So, lovers dream a rich and long delight,
   But get a winter-seeming summer's night.

Our ease, our thrift, our honour, and our day,
Shall we, for this vain bubble's shadow pay?
      Ends love in this, that my man,   15
Can be as happy as I can; if he can
Endure the short scorn of a bridegroom's play?
      That loving wretch that swears,
'Tis not the bodies marry, but the minds,
        Which he in her angelic finds,   20
        Would swear as justly, that he hears,
In that day's rude hoarse minstrelsy, the spheres.
   Hope not for mind in women; at their best
   Sweetness and wit, they are but mummy, possest.

The Flea

Mark but this flea, and mark in this,
How little that which thou deny'st me is;
It suck'd me first, and now sucks thee,
And in this flea, our two bloods mingled be;
Thou know'st that this cannot be said   5
A sin, nor shame, nor loss of maidenhead,
    Yet this enjoys before it woo,
    And pamper'd swells with one blood made of two,
    And this, alas, is more than we would do.

Oh stay, three lives in one flea spare,   10
Where we almost, nay more than married are.
This flea is you and I, and this
Our marriage bed, and marriage temple is;
Though parents grudge, and you, we're met,
And cloistered in these living walls of jet.   15
    Though use make you apt to kill me,
    Let not to that, self murder added be,
    And sacrilege, three sins in killing three.

Cruel and sudden, hast thou since
Purpled thy nail, in blood of innocence?   20
In what could this flea guilty be,
Except in that drop which it suck'd from thee?
Yet thou triumph'st, and say'st that thou
Find'st not thyself, nor me the weaker now;
    'Tis true, then learn how false, fears be;   25
    Just so much honour, when thou yield'st to me,
    Will waste, as this flea's death took life from thee.

The Curse

Whoever guesses, thinks, or dreams he knows
Who is my mistress, wither by this curse;
    His only, and only his purse
    May some dull heart to love dispose,
And she yield then to all that are his foes;   5
  May he be scorn'd by one, whom all else scorn,
  Forswear to others, what to her he hath sworn,
  With fear of missing, shame of getting, torn:

Madness his sorrow, gout his cramp, may he
Make, by but thinking who hath made him such: 10
    And may he feel no touch
    Of conscience, but of fame, and be
Anguish'd not that 'twas sin, but that 'twas she:
  In early and long scarceness may he rot,
  For land which had been his, if he had not   15
  Himself incestuously an heir begot:

May he dream treason, and believe, that he
Meant to perform it, and confess, and die,
    And no record tell why:
    His sons, which none of his may be,   20
Inherit nothing but his infamy:
  Or may he so long parasites have fed,
  That he would fain be theirs, whom he hath bred,
  And at the last be circumcis'd for bread:

The venom of all stepdames, gamesters' gall,   25
What tyrants, and their subjects interwish,
    What plants, mines, beasts, fowl, fish
    Can contribute, all ill which all
Prophets, or poets spake; and all which shall
  Be annex'd in schedules unto this by me,   30
  Fall on that man; for if it be a she
  Nature beforehand hath out-cursed me.

The Message

Send home my long stray'd eyes to me,
Which O! too long have dwelt on thee;
Yet since there they have learn'd such ill,
    Such forc'd fashions,
    And false passions,   5
        That they be
        Made by thee
Fit for no good sight, keep them still.

Send home my harmless heart again,
Which no unworthy thought could stain;   10
But if it be taught by thine
    To make jestings
    Of protestings,
        And cross both
        Word and oath,   15
Keep it, for then 'tis none of mine.

Yet send me back my heart and eyes,
That I may know, and see thy lies,
And may laugh and joy, when thou
    Art in anguish
    And dost languish   20
        For some one
        That will none,
Or prove as false as thou art now.

A Nocturnal upon St Lucy's Day,

Being the shortest day

'Tis the year's midnight, and it is the day's,
Lucy's, who scarce seven hours herself unmasks;
   The sun is spent, and now his flasks
   Send forth light squibs, no constant rays;
      The world's whole sap is sunk: 5
The general balm th' hydroptic earth hath drunk,
Whither, as to the bed's-feet, life is shrunk,
Dead and interr'd; yet all these seem to laugh,
Compar'd with me, who am their epitaph.

Study me then, you who shall lovers be   10
At the next world, that is, at the next spring:
   For I am every dead thing,
   In whom love wrought new alchemy.
      For his art did express
A quintessence even from nothingness,   15
From dull privations, and lean emptiness:
He ruin'd me, and I am re-begot
Of absence, darkness, death; things which are not.

All others, from all things, draw all that's good,
Life, soul, form, spirit, whence they being have;   20
   I, by love's limbeck, am the grave
   Of all, that's nothing. Oft a flood
      Have we two wept, and so
Drown'd the whole world, us two; oft did we grow
To be two chaoses, when we did show   25
Care to aught else; and often absences
Withdrew our souls, and made us carcasses.

But I am by her death (which word wrongs her)
Of the first nothing, the elixir grown;
   Were I a man, that I were one,   30
   I needs must know; I should prefer,

    If I were any beast,
Some ends, some means; yea plants, yea stones detest,
And love; all, all some properties invest;
If I an ordinary nothing were,   35
As shadow, a light, and body must be here.

But I am none; nor will my sun renew.
You lovers, for whose sake, the lesser sun
   At this time to the Goat is run
   To fetch new lust, and give it you,   40
      Enjoy your summer all;
Since she enjoys her long night's festival,
Let me prepare towards her, and let me call
This hour her vigil, and her eve, since this
Both the year's, and the day's deep midnight is.   45

Witchcraft by a Picture

I fix mine eye on thine, and there
   Pity my picture burning in thine eye,
My picture drown'd in a transparent tear,
   When I look lower I espy;
     Hadst thou the wicked skill   5
By pictures made and marr'd, to kill,
How many ways mightst thou perform thy will?

But now I have drunk thy sweet salt tears,
   And though thou pour more I'll depart;
My picture vanish'd, vanish fears,   10
   That I can be endamag'd by that art;
     Though thou retain of me
One picture more, yet that will be,
Being in thine own heart, from all malice free.

The Bait

Come live with me, and be my love,
And we will some new pleasures prove
Of golden sands, and crystal brooks,
With silken lines, and silver hooks.

There will the river whispering run   5
Warm'd by thy eyes, more than the sun.
And there th' enamour'd fish will stay,
Begging themselves they may betray.

When thou wilt swim in that live bath,
Each fish, which every channel hath,   10
Will amorously to thee swim,
Gladder to catch thee, than thou him.

If thou, to be so seen, be'st loth,
By sun, or moon, thou dark'nest both,
And if myself have leave to see,   15
I need not their light, having thee.

Let others freeze with angling reeds,
And cut their legs, with shells and weeds,
Or treacherously poor fish beset,
With strangling snare, or windowy net: 20

Let coarse bold hands, from slimy nest
The bedded fish in banks out-wrest,
Or curious traitors, sleave-silk flies
Bewitch poor fishes' wand'ring eyes.

For thee, thou need'st no such deceit,   25
For thou thyself art thine own bait;
That fish, that is not catch'd thereby,
Alas, is wiser far than I.

The Apparition

When by thy scorn, O murd'ress, I am dead,
And that thou think'st thee free
From all solicitation from me,
Then shall my ghost come to thy bed,
And thee, feign'd vestal, in worse arms shall see;   5
Then thy sick taper will begin to wink,
And he, whose thou art then, being tir'd before,
Will, if thou stir, or pinch to wake him, think
    Thou call'st for more,
And in false sleep will from thee shrink,   10
And then poor aspen wretch, neglected thou
Bath'd in a cold quicksilver sweat wilt lie
    A verier ghost than I;
What I will say, I will not tell thee now,
Lest that preserve thee; and since my love is spent,   15
I'd rather thou shouldst painfully repent,
Than by my threat'nings rest still innocent.

The Broken Heart

He is stark mad, who ever says,
   That he hath been in love an hour,
Yet not that love so soon decays,
   But that it can ten in less space devour;
Who will believe me, if I swear   5
That I have had the plague a year?
   Who would not laugh at me, if I should say,
   I saw a flask of powder burn a day?

Ah, what a trifle is a heart,
   If once into Love's hands it come!   10
All other griefs allow a part
   To other griefs, and ask themselves but some;
They come to us, but us Love draws,
He swallows us, and never chaws:
   By him, as by chain'd shot, whole ranks do die,   15
   He is the tyrant pike, our hearts the fry.

If 'twere not so, what did become
   Of my heart, when I first saw thee?
I brought a heart into the room,
   But from the room, I carried none with me: 20
If it had gone to thee, I know
Mine would have taught thine heart to show
   More pity unto me: but Love, alas,
   At one first blow did shiver it as glass.

Yet nothing can to nothing fall,   25
   Nor any place be empty quite,
Therefore I think my breast hath all
   Those pieces still, though they be not unite;
And now as broken glasses show
A hundred lesser faces, so   30
   My rags of heart can like, wish, and adore,
   But after one such love, can love no more.

A Valediction: Forbidding Mourning

As virtuous men pass mildly away,
    And whisper to their souls, to go,
Whilst some of their sad friends do say,
    The breath goes now, and some say, no:

So let us melt, and make no noise, 5
    No tear-floods, nor sigh-tempests move,
'Twere profanation of our joys
    To tell the laity our love.

Moving of th' earth brings harms and fears,
    Men reckon what it did and meant, 10
But trepidation of the spheres,
    Though greater far, is innocent.

Dull sublunary lovers' love
    (Whose soul is sense) cannot admit
Absence, because it doth remove 15
    Those things which elemented it.

But we by a love, so much refin'd,
    That ourselves know not what it is,
Inter-assured of the mind,
    Care less eyes, lips, and hands to miss. 20

Our two souls therefore, which are one,
    Though I must go, endure not yet
A breach, but an expansion,
    Like gold to airy thinness beat.

If they be two, they are two so 25
    As stiff twin compasses are two,
Thy soul the fix'd foot, makes no show
    To move, but doth, if th' other do.

And though it in the centre sit,
    Yet when the other far doth roam, 30
It leans, and hearkens after it,
    And grows erect, as that comes home.

Such wilt thou be to me, who must
    Like th' other foot, obliquely run;
Thy firmness makes my circle just,
    And makes me end, where I begun. 35

The Ecstasy

Where, like a pillow on a bed,
   A pregnant bank swell'd up, to rest
The violet's reclining head,
   Sat we two, one another's best.

Our hands were firmly cemented   5
   With a fast balm, which thence did spring,
Our eye-beams twisted, and did thread
   Our eyes, upon one double string;

So t' intergraft our hands, as yet
   Was all the means to make us one,   10
And pictures in our eyes to get
   Was all our propagation.

As 'twixt two equal armies, Fate
   Suspends uncertain victory,
Our souls (which to advance their state,   15
   Were gone out) hung 'twixt her, and me.

And whilst our souls negotiate there,
   We like sepulchral statues lay;
All day, the same our postures were,
   And we said nothing, all the day.   20

If any, so by love refin'd,
   That he soul's language understood,
And by good love were grown all mind,
   Within convenient distance stood,

He (though he knew not which soul spake,   25
   Because both meant, both spake the same)
Might thence a new concoction take,
   And part far purer than he came.

This ecstasy doth unperplex
   (We said) and tell us what we love,   30
We see by this, it was not sex,
   We see, we saw not what did move:

But as all several souls contain
   Mixture of things, they know not what,
Love these mix'd souls doth mix again,   35
   And makes both one, each this and that.

A single violet transplant,
   The strength, the colour, and the size
(All which before was poor, and scant)
   Redoubles still, and multiplies.   40

When love, with one another so
   Interinanimates two souls,
That abler soul, which thence doth flow,
   Defects of loneliness controls.

We then, who are this new soul, know,   45
   Of what we are compos'd, and made,
For, th' atomies of which we grow,
   Are souls, whom no change can invade.

But O alas, so long, so far
   Our bodies why do we forbear?   50
They are ours, though they are not we, we are
   The intelligences, they the sphere.

We owe them thanks, because they thus,
   Did us, to us, at first convey,
Yielded their forces, sense, to us,   55
   Nor are dross to us, but allay.

On man heaven's influence works not so,
   But that it first imprints the air,
So soul into the soul may flow,
   Though it to body first repair.   60

As our blood labours to beget
   Spirits, as like souls as it can,
Because such fingers need to knit
   That subtle knot, which makes us man:

So must pure lovers' souls descend   65
   T' affections, and to faculties,
Which sense may reach and apprehend,
   Else a great prince in prison lies.

To our bodies turn we then, that so
   Weak men on love reveal'd may look;   70
Love's mysteries in souls do grow,
   But yet the body is his book.

And if some lover, such as we,
   Have heard this dialogue of one,
Let him still mark us, he shall see   75
   Small change, when we're to bodies gone.

Love's Deity

I long to talk with some old lover's ghost,
   Who died before the god of Love was born:
I cannot think that he, who then lov'd most,
   Sunk so low, as to love one which did scorn.
But since this god produc'd a destiny,   5
And that vice-nature, custom, lets it be:
   I must love her, that loves not me.

Sure, they which made him god, meant not so much,
   Nor he, in his young godhead practis'd it.
But when an even flame two hearts did touch,   10
   His office was indulgently to fit
Actives to passives. Correspondency
Only his subject was; it cannot be
   Love, till I love her, that loves me.

But every modern god will now extend   15
   His vast prerogative, as far as Jove.
To rage, to lust, to write to, to commend,
   All is the purlieu of the god of Love.
Oh were we waken'd by this tyranny
To ungod this child again, it could not be   20
   I should love her, who loves not me.

Rebel and atheist too, why murmur I,
   As though I felt the worst that love could do?
Love might make me leave loving, or might try
   A deeper plague, to make her love me too,   25
Which, since she loves before, I'm loth to see;
Falsehood is worse than hate; and that must be,
   If she whom I love, should love me.

The Will

Before I sigh my last gasp, let me breathe,
Great Love, some legacies; here I bequeath
Mine eyes to Argus, if mine eyes can see,
If they be blind, then Love, I give them thee;
My tongue to fame; to ambassadors mine ears;   5
    To women or the sea, my tears.
Thou, Love, hast taught me heretofore
 By making me serve her who had twenty more,
That I should give to none, but such, as had too much before.

My constancy I to the planets give;   10
My truth to them, who at the Court do live;
Mine ingenuity and openness,
To Jesuits; to buffoons my pensiveness;
My silence to any, who abroad hath been;
    My money to a Capuchin.   15
Thou Love taught'st me, by appointing me
 To love there, where no love receiv'd can be,
Only to give to such as have an incapacity.

My faith I give to Roman Catholics;
All my good works unto the schismatics   20
Of Amsterdam: my best civility
And courtship, to an university;
My modesty I give to soldiers bare;
    My patience let gamesters share.
Thou Love taught'st me, by making me   25
 Love her that holds my love disparity,
Only to give to those that count my gifts indignity.

I give my reputation to those
Which were my friends; mine industry to foes;
To schoolmen I bequeath my doubtfulness;   30
My sickness to physicians, or excess;
To Nature, all that I in rhyme have writ;

And to my company my wit.
Thou Love, by making me adore
Her, who begot this love in me before,   35
Taught'st me to make, as though I gave, when I did but restore.

To him for whom the passing bell next tolls,
I give my physic books; my written rolls
Of moral counsels, I to Bedlam give;
My brazen medals, unto them which live   40
In want of bread; to them which pass among
All foreigners, mine English tongue.
Thou, Love, by making me love one
Who thinks her friendship a fit portion
For younger lovers, dost my gifts thus disproportion.   45

Therefore I'll give no more; but I'll undo
The world by dying; because love dies too.
Then all your beauties will be no more worth
Than gold in mines, where none doth draw it forth;
And all your graces no more use shall have   50
Than a sundial in a grave.
Thou Love taught'st me, by making me
Love her, who doth neglect both me and thee,
To invent, and practise this one way, to annihilate all three.

The Funeral

Whoever comes to shroud me, do not harm
      Nor question much
That subtle wreath of hair, which crowns my arm;
The mystery, the sign you must not touch,
      For 'tis my outward soul,   5
Viceroy to that, which then to heaven being gone,
      Will leave this to control,
And keep these limbs, her provinces, from dissolution.

For if the sinewy thread my brain lets fall
      Through every part,   10
Can tie those parts, and make me one of all,
These hairs which upward grew, and strength and art
      Have from a better brain,
Can better do 't; except she meant that I
      By this should know my pain,   15
As prisoners then are manacled, when they're condemn'd
      to die.

Whate'er she meant by it, bury it with me,
      For since I am
Love's martyr, it might breed idolatry,
If into others' hand these relics came;
      As 'twas humility   20
To afford to it all that a soul can do,
      So, 'tis some bravery,
That since you would save none of me, I bury some of you.

The Blossom

Little think'st thou, poor flower,
  Whom I have watched six or seven days,
And seen thy birth, and seen what every hour
Gave to thy growth, thee to this height to raise,
And now dost laugh and triumph on this bough,   5
       Little think'st thou
That it will freeze anon, and that I shall
Tomorrow find thee fall'n, or not at all.

Little think'st thou, poor heart,
  That labour'st yet to nestle thee,   10
And think'st by hovering here to get a part
In a forbidden or forbidding tree,
And hop'st her stiffness by long siege to bow:
       Little think'st thou,
That thou tomorrow, ere that sun doth wake,   15
Must with this sun, and me a journey take.

But thou which lov'st to be
  Subtle to plague thyself, wilt say,
Alas, if you must go, what's that to me?
Here lies my business, and here I will stay: 20
You go to friends, whose love and means present
       Various content
To your eyes, ears, and tongue, and every part.
If then your body go, what need you a heart?

Well then, stay here; but know,   25
  When thou hast stay'd and done thy most,
A naked thinking heart, that makes no show,
Is to a woman, but a kind of ghost;
How shall she know my heart; or having none,
       Know thee for one?   30
Practice may make her know some other part,
But take my word, she doth not know a heart.

Meet me at London, then,
    Twenty days hence, and thou shalt see
Me fresher, and more fat, by being with men,   35
Than if I had stay'd still with her and thee.
For God's sake, if you can, be you so too:
        I would give you
There, to another friend, whom we shall find
As glad to have my body, as my mind.   40

The Relic

When my grave is broke up again
Some second guest to entertain
(For graves have learn'd that woman-head
To be to more than one a bed),
    And he that digs it, spies   5
A bracelet of bright hair about the bone,
    Will he not let us alone,
And think that there a loving couple lies,
Who thought that this device might be some way
To make their souls, at the last busy day,   10
Meet at this grave, and make a little stay?

If this fall in a time, or land,
Where mis-devotion doth command,
Then, he that digs us up, will bring
Us, to the Bishop, and the King,   15
    To make us relics; then
Thou shalt be a Mary Magdalene, and I
    A something else thereby;
All women shall adore us, and some men;
And since at such time, miracles are sought,   20
I would have that age by this paper taught
What miracles we harmless lovers wrought.

First, we lov'd well and faithfully,
Yet knew not what we lov'd, nor why,
Difference of sex no more we knew,   25
Than our guardian angels do;
    Coming and going, we
Perchance might kiss, but not between those meals;
    Our hands ne'er touched the seals,
Which nature, injur'd by late law, sets free: 30
These miracles we did; but now alas,
All measure, and all language, I should pass,
Should I tell what a miracle she was.

The Prohibition

Take heed of loving me,
At least remember, I forbade it thee;
Not that I shall repair my unthrifty waste
Of breath and blood, upon thy sighs, and tears,
By being to thee then what to me thou wast;   5
But, so great joy our life at once outwears,
Then, lest thy love, by my death, frustrate be,
If thou love me, take heed of loving me.

Take heed of hating me,
Or too much triumph in the victory.   10
Not that I shall be mine own officer,
And hate with hate again retaliate;
But thou wilt lose the style of conqueror,
If I, thy conquest, perish by thy hate.
Then, lest my being nothing lessen thee,   15
If thou hate me, take heed of hating me.

Yet, love and hate me too,
So, these extremes shall neither's office do;
Love me, that I may die the gentler way;
Hate me, because thy love's too great for me;   20
Or let these two, themselves, not me decay;
So shall I, live, thy stage, not triumph be;
Lest thou thy love and hate and me undo,
To let me live, Oh love and hate me too.

The Expiration

So, so, break off this last lamenting kiss,
   Which sucks two souls, and vapours both away;
Turn thou ghost that way, and let me turn this,
   And let ourselves benight our happiest day;
We ask'd none leave to love; nor will we owe   5
   Any, so cheap a death, as saying, Go;

Go; and if that word have not quite killed thee,
   Ease me with death, by bidding me go too.
Oh, if it have, let my word work on me,
   And a just office on a murderer do.   10
Except it be too late, to kill me so,
   Being double dead, going, and bidding, Go.

The Computation

For the first twenty years, since yesterday,
   I scarce believ'd, thou could'st be gone away,
For forty more, I fed on favours past,
   And forty on hopes, that thou would'st, they might last.
Tears drown'd one hundred, and sighs blew out two,   5
   A thousand, I did neither think, nor do,
   Or not divide, all being one thought of you;
   Or in a thousand more, forgot that too.
Yet call not this long life; but think that I
Am, by being dead, immortal; can ghosts die?   10

Elegies

Elegy 5

His Picture

Here take my picture; though I bid farewell,
Thine, in my heart, where my soul dwells, shall dwell.
'Tis like me now, but I dead, 'twill be more
When we are shadows both, than 'twas before.
When weather-beaten I come back; my hand,   5
Perhaps with rude oars torn, or sun-beams tann'd,
My face and breast of haircloth, and my head
With care's rash sudden storms being o'erspread,
My body a sack of bones, broken within,
And powder's blue stains scatter'd on my skin;   10
If rival fools tax thee to have lov'd a man,
So foul, and coarse, as oh, I may seem then,
This shall say what I was: and thou shalt say,
Do his hurts reach me? doth my worth decay?
Or do they reach his judging mind, that he   15
Should now love less, what he did love to see?
That which in him was fair and delicate,
Was but the milk, which in love's childish state
Did nurse it: who now is grown strong enough
To feed on that, which to disus'd tastes seems tough.   20

Elegy 9

The Autumnal

No spring, nor summer beauty hath such grace,
    As I have seen in one autumnal face.
Young beauties force your love, and that's a rape,
    This doth but counsel, yet you cannot 'scape.
If 'twere a shame to love, here 'twere no shame,   5
    Affection here takes reverence's name.
Were her first years the Golden Age; that's true,
    But now she's gold oft tried, and ever new.
That was her torrid and inflaming time,
    This is her tolerable tropic clime.   10
Fair eyes, who asks more heat than comes from hence,
    He in a fever wishes pestilence.
Call not these wrinkles, graves; if graves they were,
    They were Love's graves; for else he is no where.
Yet lies not Love dead here, but here doth sit   15
    Vow'd to this trench, like an anachorit,
And here, till hers, which must be his death, come,
    He doth not dig a grave, but build a tomb.
Here dwells he, though he sojourn ev'rywhere,
    In progress, yet his standing house is here.   20
Here, where still evening is; not noon, nor night;
    Where no voluptuousness, yet all delight.
In all her words, unto all hearers fit,
    You may at revels, you at council, sit.
This is Love's timber, youth his underwood;   25
    There he, as wine in June, enrages blood,
Which then comes seasonabliest, when our taste
    And appetite to other things is past.
Xerxes' strange Lydian love, the platane tree,
    Was lov'd for age, none being so large as she,   30
Or else because, being young, nature did bless
    Her youth with age's glory, barrenness.
If we love things long sought, age is a thing

Which we are fifty years in compassing.
If transitory things, which soon decay,   35
   Age must be loveliest at the latest day.
But name not winter-faces, whose skin's slack;
   Lank, as an unthrift's purse; but a soul's sack;
Whose eyes seek light within, for all here's shade;
   Whose mouths are holes, rather worn out, than made;   40
Whose every tooth to a several place is gone,
   To vex their souls at Resurrection;
Name not these living death's-heads unto me,
   For these, not ancient, but antique be.
I hate extremes; yet I had rather stay   45
   With tombs, than cradles, to wear out a day.
Since such love's natural lation is, may still
   My love descend, and journey down the hill,
Not panting after growing beauties, so,
   I shall ebb out with them, who homeward go.   50

Elegy 10

The Dream

Image of her whom I love, more than she,
　　Whose fair impression in my faithful heart,
Makes me her medal, and makes her love me,
　　As kings do coins, to which their stamps impart
The value: go, and take my heart from hence,　　　　5
　　Which now is grown too great and good for me:
Honours oppress weak spirits, and our sense
　　Strong objects dull; the more, the less we see.
When you are gone, and reason gone with you,
　　Then fantasy is queen and soul, and all;　　　　10
She can present joys meaner than you do,
　　Convenient, and more proportional.
So, if I dream I have you, I have you,
　　For, all our joys are but fantastical.
And so I 'scape the pain, for pain is true;　　　　15
　　And sleep which locks up sense, doth lock out all.
After a such fruition I shall wake,
　　And, but the waking, nothing shall repent;
And shall to love more thankful sonnets make,
　　Than if more honour, tears, and pains were spent.　　20
But dearest heart, and dearer image, stay;
　　Alas, true joys at best are dream enough;
Though you stay here you pass too fast away:
　　For even at first life's taper is a snuff.
Fill'd with her love, may I be rather grown　　　　25
Mad with much heart, than idiot with none.

Elegy 16

On his Mistress

By our first strange and fatal interview,
By all desires which thereof did ensue,
By our long starving hopes, by that remorse
Which my words' masculine persuasive force
Begot in thee, and by the memory   5
Of hurts, which spies and rivals threatened me,
I calmly beg: but by thy father's wrath,
By all pains, which want and divorcement hath,
I conjure thee, and all the oaths which I
And thou have sworn to seal joint constancy,   10
Here I unswear, and overswear them thus:
Thou shalt not love by ways so dangerous.
Temper, O fair love, love's impetuous rage,
Be my true mistress still, not my feign'd page.
I'll go, and, by thy kind leave, leave behind   15
Thee, only worthy to nurse in my mind
Thirst to come back; O if thou die before,
My soul from other lands to thee shall soar.
Thy (else almighty) beauty cannot move
Rage from the seas, nor thy love teach them love,   20
Nor tame wild Boreas' harshness; thou hast read
How roughly he in pieces shivered
Fair Orithea, whom he swore he lov'd.
Fall ill or good, 'tis madness to have prov'd
Dangers unurg'd; feed on this flattery,   25
That absent lovers one in th' other be.
Dissemble nothing, not a boy, nor change
Thy body's habit, nor mind's; be not strange
To thy self only; all will spy in thy face
A blushing womanly discovering grace.   30
Richly cloth'd apes, are call'd apes, and as soon
Eclips'd as bright we call the moon the moon.
Men of France, changeable chameleons,

Spitals of diseases, shops of fashions,
Love's fuellers, and the rightest company   35
Of players, which upon the world's stage be,
Will quickly know thee, and no less, alas!
Th' indifferent Italian, as we pass
His warm land, well content to think thee page,
Will hunt thee with such lust, and hideous rage,   40
As Lot's fair guests were vex'd. But none of these
Nor spongy hydroptic Dutch shall thee displease,
If thou stay here. O stay here, for, for thee
England is only a worthy gallery,
To walk in expectation, till from thence   45
Our greatest King call thee to his presence.
When I am gone, dream me some happiness,
Nor let thy looks our long-hid love confess,
Nor praise, nor dispraise me, nor bless nor curse
Openly love's force, nor in bed fright thy nurse   50
With midnight's startings, crying out, 'Oh, oh
Nurse, O my love is slain, I saw him go
O'er the white Alps alone; I saw him, I,
Assail'd, fight, taken, stabb'd, bleed, fall, and die.'
Augur me better chance, except dread Jove   55
Think it enough for me, to have had thy love.

Elegy 19

To his Mistress Going to Bed

Come Madam, come, all rest my powers defy,
Until I labour, I in labour lie.
The foe oft-times having the foe in sight,
Is tired with standing though he never fight.
Off with that girdle, like heaven's zone glistering,   5
But a far fairer world encompassing.
Unpin that spangled breastplate which you wear
That th' eyes of busy fools may be stopt there.
Unlace yourself, for that harmonious chime
Tells me from you, that now it is bed time.   10
Off with that happy busk, which I envy,
That still can be, and still can stand so nigh.
Your gown going off, such beauteous state reveals,
As when from flow'ry meads th' hill's shadow steals.
Off with that wiry coronet and show   15
The hairy diadem which on you doth grow.
Now off with those shoes, and then safely tread
In this love's hallow'd temple, this soft bed.
In such white robes heaven's angels used to be
Receiv'd by men; thou angel bring'st with thee   20
A heaven like Mahomet's paradise; and though
Ill spirits walk in white, we easily know
By this, these angels from an evil sprite,
Those set our hairs, but these our flesh upright.
    License my roving hands, and let them go   25
Before, behind, between, above, below.
O my America! my new-found-land,
My kingdom, safeliest when with one man mann'd,
My mine of precious stones, my empery,
How blest am I in this discovering thee!   30
To enter in these bonds, is to be free;
Then where my hand is set, my seal shall be.
    Full nakedness! All joys are due to thee;

As souls unbodied, bodies uncloth'd must be,
To taste whole joys. Gems which you women use   35
Are like Atlanta's balls, cast in men's views,
That when a fool's eye lighteth on a gem,
His earthly soul may covet theirs, not them.
Like pictures, or like books' gay coverings made
For laymen, are all women thus array'd;   40
Themselves are mystic books, which only we
(Whom their imputed grace will dignify)
Must see reveal'd. Then since that I may know,
As liberally as to a midwife show
Thyself: cast all, yea, this white linen hence,   45
Here is no penance, much less innocence.
　　To teach thee, I am naked first: why then
What needst thou have more covering than a man?

Epithalamiums

An Epithalamion, or Marriage Song

On the Lady Elizabeth and Count Palatine being
married on St Valentine's Day

1

Hail Bishop Valentine, whose day this is,
    All the air is thy diocese,
    And all the chirping choristers
And other birds are thy parishioners;
    Thou marriest every year   5
The lyric lark, and the grave whispering dove,
The sparrow that neglects his life for love,
The household bird, with the red stomacher;
    Thou mak'st the blackbird speed as soon,
As doth the goldfinch, or the halcyon;   10
The husband cock looks out, and straight is sped,
And meets his wife, which brings her feather-bed.
This day more cheerfully than ever shine,
This day, which might inflame thyself, Old Valentine.

2

Till now, thou warm'd'st with multiplying loves   15
    Two larks, two sparrows, or two doves;
    All that is nothing unto this,
For thou this day couplest two phœnixes,
    Thou mak'st a taper see
What the sun never saw, and what the Ark   20
(Which was of fowls, and beasts, the cage, and park)
Did not contain, one bed contains, through thee,
    Two phœnixes, whose joined breasts
Are unto one another mutual nests,
Where motion kindles such fires, as shall give   25
Young phœnixes, and yet the old shall live;

Whose love and courage never shall decline,
But make the whole year through, thy day, O Valentine.

3

Up then fair phœnix bride, frustrate the sun,
     Thyself from thine affection   30
     Tak'st warmth enough, and from thine eye
All lesser birds will take their jollity.
     Up, up, fair bride, and call,
Thy stars, from out their several boxes, take
Thy rubies, pearls, and diamonds forth, and make   35
Thyself a constellation, of them all,
     And by their blazing, signify,
That a great princess falls, but doth not die;
Be thou a new star, that to us portends
Ends of much wonder; and be thou those ends.   40
Since thou dost this day in new glory shine,
May all men date records, from this thy Valentine.

4

Come forth, come forth, and as one glorious flame
     Meeting another, grows the same,
     So meet thy Frederick, and so   45
To an unseparable union grow.
     Since separation
Falls not on such things as are infinite,
Nor things which are but one, can disunite,
You're twice inseparable, great, and one;   50
     Go, then to where the Bishop stays,
To make you one, his way, which divers ways
Must be effected; and when all is past,
And that you're one, by hearts and hands made fast,
You two have one way left, yourselves to entwine,   55
Besides this Bishop's knot, or Bishop Valentine.

5

But oh, what ails the sun, that here he stays,
     Longer today, than other days?
     Stays he new light from these to get?
And finding here such store, is loth to set?   60

And why do you two walk,
So slowly pac'd in this procession?
Is all your care but to be look'd upon,
And be to others spectacle, and talk?
 The feast, with gluttonous delays,   65
Is eaten, and too long their meat they praise,
The masquers come too late, and I think, will stay,
Like fairies, till the cock crow them away.
Alas, did not antiquity assign
A night, as well as day, to thee, O Valentine?   70

6

They did, and night is come; and yet we see
 Formalities retarding thee.
 What mean these ladies, which (as though
They were to take a clock in pieces) go
 So nicely about the bride;   75
A bride, before a good-night could be said,
Should vanish from her clothes, into her bed,
As souls from bodies steal, and are not spied.
 But now she is laid; what though she be?
Yet there are more delays, for, where is he?   80
He comes, and passes through sphere after sphere,
First her sheets, then her arms, then any where.
Let not this day, then, but this night be thine,
Thy day was but the eve to this, O Valentine.

7

Here lies a she sun, and a he moon here,   85
 She gives the best light to his sphere,
 Or each is both, and all, and so
They unto one another nothing owe,
 And yet they do, but are
So just and rich in that coin, which they pay,   90
That neither would, nor needs forbear nor stay;
Neither desires to be spar'd, nor to spare,
 They quickly pay their debt, and then
Take no acquittances, but pay again;
They pay, they give, they lend, and so let fall   95
No such occasion to be liberal.

More truth, more courage in these two do shine,
Than all thy turtles have, and sparrows, Valentine.

8

And by this act of these two phœnixes
    Nature again restored is,   100
    For since these two are two no more,
There's but one phœnix still, as was before.
    Rest now at last, and we
As satyrs watch the sun's uprise, will stay
Waiting, when your eyes open'd, let out day,   105
Only desir'd, because your face we see;
    Others near you shall whispering speak,
And wagers lay, at which side day will break,
And win by observing, then, whose hand it is
That opens first a curtain, hers or his;   110
This will be tried tomorrow after nine,
Till which hour, we thy day enlarge, O Valentine.

Epithalamion made at Lincoln's Inn

The sun-beams in the east are spread,
Leave, leave, fair bride, your solitary bed,
   No more shall you return to it alone,
It nurseth sadness, and your body's print,
Like to a grave, the yielding down doth dint;   5
   You and your other you meet there anon;
     Put forth, put forth that warm balm-breathing thigh,
Which when next time you in these sheets will smother,
There it must meet another,
   Which never was, but must be, oft, more nigh;   10
Come glad from thence, go gladder than you came,
Today put on perfection, and a woman's name.

Daughters of London, you which be
Our golden mines, and furnish'd treasury,
   You which are angels, yet still bring with you   15
Thousands of angels on your marriage days,
Help with your presence and device to praise
   These rites, which also unto you grow due;
     Conceitedly dress her, and be assign'd,
By you, fit place for every flower and jewel,   20
Make her for love fit fuel;
   As gay as Flora, and as rich as Ind;
So may she fair, rich, glad, and in nothing lame,
Today put on perfection, and a woman's name.

And you frolic patricians,   25
Sons of these senators' wealth's deep oceans,
   Ye painted courtiers, barrels of others' wits,
Ye country men, who but your beasts love none,
Ye of those fellowships whereof he's one,
   Of study and play made strange hermaphrodites,   30
     Here shine; this bridegroom to the temple bring.
Lo, in yon path which store of strew'd flowers graceth,
The sober virgin paceth;

Except my sight fail, 'tis no other thing;
Weep not nor blush, here is no grief nor shame,   35
Today put on perfection, and a woman's name.

Thy two-leav'd gates, fair temple, unfold,
And these two in thy sacred bosom hold,
    Till, mystically join'd, but one they be;
Then may thy lean and hunger-starved womb   40
Long time expect their bodies and their tomb,
    Long after their own parents fatten thee.
        All elder claims, and all cold barrenness,
All yielding to new loves be far for ever,
Which might these two dissever,   45
    All ways, all th' other may each one possess;
For, the best bride, best worthy of praise and fame,
Today puts on perfection, and a woman's name.

Oh winter days bring much delight,
Not for themselves, but for they soon bring night;   50
    Other sweets wait thee than these diverse meats,
Other disports than dancing jollities,
Other love tricks than glancing with the eyes,
    But that the sun still in our half sphere sweats;
        He flies in winter, but he now stands still.   55
Yet shadows turn; noon point he hath attain'd,
His steeds nill be restrain'd,
    But gallop lively down the western hill;
Thou shalt, when he hath run the world's half frame,
Tonight put on perfection, and a woman's name.   60

The amorous evening star is rose,
Why then should not our amorous star inclose
    Herself in her wish'd bed? Release your strings,
Musicians, and dancers take some truce
With these your pleasing labours, for great use   65
    As much weariness as perfection brings;
        You, and not only you, but all toil'd beasts
Rest duly; at night all their toils are dispens'd;
But in their beds commenc'd
    Are other labours, and more dainty feasts;   70

She goes a maid, who, lest she turn the same,
Tonight puts on perfection, and a woman's name.

Thy virgin's girdle now untie,
And in thy nuptial bed (love's altar) lie
    A pleasing sacrifice; now dispossess   75
Thee of these chains and robes which were put on
T'adorn the day, not thee; for thou, alone,
    Like virtue and truth, art best in nakedness;
      This bed is only to virginity
A grave, but, to a better state, a cradle;   80
Till now thou wast but able
    To be what now thou art; then that by thee
No more be said, *I may be,* but, *I am,*
Tonight put on perfection, and a woman's name.

Even like a faithful man content,   85
That this life for a better should be spent,
    So, she a mother's rich style doth prefer,
And at the bridegroom's wish'd approach doth lie,
Like an appointed lamb, when tenderly
    The priest comes on his knees t' embowel her;   90
      Now sleep or watch with more joy; and O light
Of heaven, tomorrow rise thou hot, and early;
This sun will love so dearly
      Her rest, that long, long we shall want her sight;
Wonders are wrought, for she which had no maim,   95
Tonight puts on perfection, and a woman's name.

Satires

Satire 3

Kind pity chokes my spleen; brave scorn forbids
Those tears to issue which swell my eye-lids;
I must not laugh, nor weep sins, and be wise,
Can railing then cure these worn maladies?
Is not our mistress fair religion,   5
As worthy of all our soul's devotion,
As virtue was to the first blinded age?
Are not heaven's joys as valiant to assuage
Lusts, as earth's honour was to them? Alas,
As we do them in means, shall they surpass   10
Us in the end, and shall thy father's spirit
Meet blind philosophers in heaven, whose merit
Of strict life may be imputed faith, and hear
Thee, whom he taught so easy ways and near
To follow, damn'd? O if thou dar'st, fear this;   15
This fear great courage, and high valour is.
Dar'st thou aid mutinous Dutch, and dar'st thou lay
Thee in ships' wooden sepulchres, a prey
To leaders' rage, to storms, to shot, to dearth?
Dar'st thou dive seas, and dungeons of the earth?   20
Hast thou courageous fire to thaw the ice
Of frozen north discoveries? and thrice
Colder than salamanders, like divine
Children in th' oven, fires of Spain, and the line,
Whose countries limbecks to our bodies be,   25
Canst thou for gain bear? and must every he
Which cries not, 'Goddess!' to thy mistress, draw,
Or eat thy poisonous words? courage of straw!
O desperate coward, wilt thou seem bold, and
To thy foes and his (who made thee to stand   30
Sentinel in his world's garrison) thus yield,
And for the forbidden wars, leave th' appointed field?

Know thy foes: the foul Devil (he whom thou
Strivest to please) for hate, not love, would allow
Thee fain, his whole realm to be quit; and as   35
The world's all parts wither away and pass,
So the world's self, thy other lov'd foe, is
In her decrepit wane, and thou loving this,
Dost love a withered and worn strumpet; last,
Flesh (itself's death) and joys which flesh can taste,   40
Thou lovest; and thy fair goodly soul, which doth
Give this flesh power to taste joy, thou dost loathe.
Seek true religion. O where? Mirreus
Thinking her unhous'd here, and fled from us,
Seeks her at Rome; there, because he doth know   45
That she was there a thousand years ago;
He loves her rags so, as we here obey
The statecloth where the prince sat yesterday.
Crants to such brave loves will not be enthrall'd,
But loves her only, who at Geneva is call'd   50
Religion, plain, simple, sullen, young,
Contemptuous, yet unhandsome; as among
Lecherous humours, there is one that judges
No wenches wholesome, but coarse country drudges.
Graius stays still at home here, and because   55
Some preachers, vile ambitious bawds, and laws
Still new like fashions, bid him think that she
Which dwells with us, is only perfect, he
Embraceth her, whom his godfathers will
Tender to him, being tender, as wards still   60
Take such wives as their guardians offer, or
Pay values. Careless Phrygius doth abhor
All, because all cannot be good, as one
Knowing some women whores, dares marry none.
Gracchus loves all as one, and thinks that so   65
As women do in divers countries go
In divers habits, yet are still one kind,
So doth, so is religion; and this blind-
ness too much light breeds; but unmoved thou
Of force must one, and forc'd but one allow;   70
And the right; ask thy father which is she,
Let him ask his; though truth and falsehood be

Near twins, yet truth a little elder is;
Be busy to seek her, believe me this,
He's not of none, nor worst, that seeks the best.   75
To adore, or scorn an image, or protest,
May all be bad; doubt wisely; in strange way
To stand inquiring right, is not to stray;
To sleep, or run wrong, is. On a huge hill,
Cragged, and steep, Truth stands, and he that will   80
Reach her, about must, and about must go;
And what the hill's suddenness resists, win so;
Yet strive so, that before age, death's twilight,
Thy soul rest, for none can work in that night.
To will, implies delay, therefore now do: 85
Hard deeds, the body's pains; hard knowledge too
The mind's endeavours reach, and mysteries
Are like the sun, dazzling, yet plain to all eyes.
Keep the truth which thou hast found; men do not stand
In so ill case here, that God hath with his hand   90
Sign'd kings blank-charters to kill whom they hate,
Nor are they vicars, but hangmen to Fate.
Fool and wretch, wilt thou let thy soul be tied
To man's laws, by which she shall not be tried
At the last day? Will it then boot thee   95
To say a Philip, or a Gregory,
A Harry, or a Martin taught thee this?
Is not this excuse for mere contraries,
Equally strong? cannot both sides say so?
That thou mayest rightly obey power, her bounds know;   100
Those past, her nature and name is chang'd; to be
Then humble to her is idolatry.
As streams are, power is; those blest flowers that dwell
At the rough stream's calm head, thrive and do well,
But having left their roots, and themselves given   105
To the stream's tyrannous rage, alas are driven
Through mills, and rocks, and woods, and at last, almost
Consum'd in going, in the sea are lost:
So perish souls, which more choose men's unjust
Power from God claim'd, than God himself to trust.   110

Verse Letters

To Sir Henry Wotton

Here's no more news, than virtue, I may as well
Tell you Cadiz' or Saint Michael's tale for news, as tell
That vice doth here habitually dwell.

Yet, as to get stomachs, we walk up and down,
And toil to sweeten rest, so, may God frown,   5
If, but to loathe both, I haunt Court, or Town.

For here no one is from th'extremity
Of vice, by any other reason free,
But that the next to him, still, is worse than he.

In this world's warfare, they whom rugged Fate   10
(God's commissary) doth so throughly hate,
As in the Court's squadron to marshal their state;

If they stand arm'd with silly honesty,
With wishing prayers, and neat integrity,
Like Indian 'gainst Spanish hosts they be.   15

Suspicious boldness to this place belongs,
And to have as many ears as all have tongues;
Tender to know, tough to acknowledge wrongs.

Believe me, Sir, in my youth's giddiest days,
When to be like the Court, was a play's praise,   20
Plays were not so like Courts, as Courts are like plays.

Then let us at these mimic antics jest,
Whose deepest projects, and egregious gests
Are but dull morals of a game at chests.

But now 'tis incongruity to smile,   25
Therefore I end; and bid farewell a while,
At Court, though *From Court*, were the better style.

To Mr I. L.

Of that short roll of friends writ in my heart
   Which with thy name begins, since their depart,
Whether in the English Provinces they be,
   Or drink of Po, Sequan, or Danuby,
There's none that sometimes greets us not, and yet   5
   Your Trent is Lethe; that past, us you forget.
You do not duties of societies,
   If from the embrace of a lov'd wife you rise,
View your fat beasts, stretch'd barns, and labour'd fields,
   Eat, play, ride, take all joys which all day yields,   10
And then again to your embracements go:
   Some hours on us your friends, and some bestow
Upon your Muse, else both we shall repent,
   I that my love, she that her gifts on you are spent.

To the Countess of Bedford

Honour is so sublime perfection,
And so refin'd, that when God was alone
And creatureless at first, himself had none;

But as of the elements, these which we tread,
Produce all things with which we're joy'd or fed,   5
And, those are barren both above our head:

So from low persons doth all honour flow;
Kings, whom they would have honoured, to us show,
And but direct our honour, not bestow.

For when from herbs the pure part must be won   10
From gross, by stilling, this is better done
By despis'd dung, than by the fire or sun.

Care not then, Madam, how low your praisers lie;
In labourers' ballads oft more piety
God finds, than in *Te Deums*' melody.   15

And, ordnance rais'd on towers so many mile
Send not their voice, nor last so long a while
As fires from th' earth's low vaults in Sicil Isle.

Should I say I liv'd darker than were true,
Your radiation can all clouds subdue;   20
But one, 'tis best light to contemplate you.

You, for whose body God made better clay,
Or took soul's stuff such as shall late decay,
Or such as needs small change at the last day.

This, as an amber drop enwraps a bee,   25
Covering discovers your quick soul; that we
May in your through-shine front your heart's thoughts see.

You teach (though we learn not) a thing unknown
To our late times, the use of specular stone,
Through which all things within without were shown.   30

Of such were temples; so and of such you are;
Being and seeming is your equal care,
And virtue's whole sum is but know and dare.

But as our souls of growth and souls of sense
Have birthright of our reason's soul, yet hence   35
They fly not from that, nor seek precedence:

Nature's first lesson, so, discretion,
Must not grudge zeal a place, nor yet keep none,
Not banish itself, nor religion.

Discretion is a wise man's soul, and so   40
Religion is a Christian's, and you know
How these are one; her *yea*, is not her *no*.

Nor may we hope to solder still and knit
These two, and dare to break them; nor must wit
Be colleague to religion, but be it.   45

In those poor types of God (round circles) so
Religion's types, the pieceless centres flow,
And are in all the lines which all ways go.

If either ever wrought in you alone
Or principally, then religion   50
Wrought your ends, and your ways discretion.

Go thither still, go the same way you went,
Who so would change, do covet or repent;
Neither can reach you, great and innocent.

Divine Poems

To the Lady Magdalen Herbert:
of St Mary Magdalene

Her of your name, whose fair inheritance
   Bethina was, and jointure Magdalo:
An active faith so highly did advance,
   That she once knew, more than the Church did know,
The Resurrection; so much good there is   5
   Deliver'd of her, that some Fathers be
Loth to believe one woman could do this;
   But, think these Magdalenes were two or three.
Increase their number, Lady, and their fame:
   To their devotion, add your innocence;   10
Take so much of th' example, as of the name;
The latter half; and in some recompense
That they did harbour Christ himself, a guest,
   Harbour these hymns, to his dear name address'd.

Holy Sonnets

1

Thou hast made me, and shall thy work decay?
Repair me now, for now mine end doth haste,
I run to death, and death meets me as fast,
And all my pleasures are like yesterday;
I dare not move my dim eyes any way,   5
Despair behind, and death before doth cast
Such terror, and my feeble flesh doth waste
By sin in it, which it towards hell doth weigh;
Only thou art above, and when towards thee
By thy leave I can look, I rise again;   10
But our old subtle foe so tempteth me,
That not one hour myself I can sustain;
Thy grace may wing me to prevent his art,
And thou like adamant draw mine iron heart.

3

O might those sighs and tears return again
Into my breast and eyes, which I have spent,
That I might in this holy discontent
Mourn with some fruit, as I have mourn'd in vain;
In mine idolatry what showers of rain   5
Mine eyes did waste? what griefs my heart did rent?
That sufferance was my sin, now I repent;
'Cause I did suffer I must suffer pain.
Th' hydroptic drunkard, and night-scouting thief,
The itchy lecher, and self-tickling proud   10
Have the remembrance of past joys, for relief
Of coming ills. To poor me is allow'd
No ease; for, long, yet vehement grief hath been
Th' effect and cause, the punishment and sin.

4

Oh my black soul! now thou art summoned
By sickness, death's herald, and champion;

Thou art like a pilgrim, which abroad hath done
Treason, and durst not turn to whence he is fled,
Or like a thief, which till death's doom be read,   5
Wisheth himself delivered from prison;
But damn'd and hal'd to execution,
Wisheth that still he might be imprisoned.
Yet grace, if thou repent, thou canst not lack;
But who shall give thee that grace to begin?   10
Oh make thyself with holy mourning black,
And red with blushing, as thou art with sin;
Or wash thee in Christ's blood, which hath this might
That being red, it dyes red souls to white.

5

I am a little world made cunningly
Of elements, and an angelic sprite,
But black sin hath betray'd to endless night
My world's both parts, and, oh, both parts must die.
You which beyond that heaven which was most high   5
Have found new spheres, and of new lands can write,
Pour new seas in mine eyes, that so I might
Drown my world with my weeping earnestly,
Or wash it if it must be drown'd no more:
But oh it must be burnt! alas the fire   10
Of lust and envy have burnt it heretofore,
And made it fouler; let their flames retire,
And burn me O Lord, with a fiery zeal
Of thee and thy house, which doth in eating heal.

6

This is my play's last scene, here heavens appoint
My pilgrimage's last mile; and my race
Idly, yet quickly run, hath this last pace,
My span's last inch, my minute's latest point,
And gluttonous death will instantly unjoint   5
My body, and soul, and I shall sleep a space,
But my ever-waking part shall see that face,
Whose fear already shakes my every joint:
Then, as my soul, to heaven her first seat, takes flight,
And earth-born body, in the earth shall dwell,   10

So, fall my sins, that all may have their right,
To where they're bred, and would press me, to hell.
Impute me righteous, thus purg'd of evil,
For thus I leave the world, the flesh, the devil.

7

At the round earth's imagin'd corners, blow
Your trumpets, angels, and arise, arise
From death, you numberless infinities
Of souls, and to your scatter'd bodies go,
All whom the flood did, and fire shall o'erthrow,   5
All whom war, dearth, age, agues, tyrannies,
Despair, law, chance, hath slain, and you whose eyes
Shall behold God, and never taste death's woe.
But let them sleep, Lord, and me mourn a space,
For, if above all these, my sins abound,   10
'Tis late to ask abundance of thy grace,
When we are there; here on this lowly ground,
Teach me how to repent; for that's as good
As if thou hadst seal'd my pardon, with thy blood.

9

If poisonous minerals, and if that tree,
Whose fruit threw death on else immortal us,
If lecherous goats, if serpents envious
Cannot be damn'd, alas why should I be?
Why should intent or reason, born in me,   5
Make sins, else equal, in me more heinous?
And mercy being easy, and glorious
To God, in his stern wrath, why threatens he?
But who am I, that dare dispute with thee
O God? Oh! of thine only worthy blood,   10
And my tears, make a heavenly Lethean flood,
And drown in it my sin's black memory;
That thou remember them, some claim as debt,
I think it mercy, if thou wilt forget.

10

Death be not proud, though some have called thee
Mighty and dreadful, for, thou art not so,

For, those, whom thou think'st thou dost overthrow,
Die not, poor death, nor yet canst thou kill me.
From rest and sleep, which but thy pictures be,   5
Much pleasure, then from thee, much more must flow,
And soonest our best men with thee do go,
Rest of their bones, and soul's delivery.
Thou art slave to fate, chance, kings, and desperate men,
And dost with poison, war, and sickness dwell,   10
And poppy, or charms can make us sleep as well,
And better than thy stroke; why swell'st thou then?
One short sleep past, we wake eternally,
And death shall be no more; death, thou shalt die.

12

Why are we by all creatures waited on?
Why do the prodigal elements supply
Life and food to me, being more pure than I,
Simple, and further from corruption?
Why brook'st thou, ignorant horse, subjection?   5
Why dost thou, bull and boar, so sillily
Dissemble weakness, and by one man's stroke die,
Whose whole kind, you might swallow and feed upon?
Weaker I am, woe is me, and worse than you,
You have not sinn'd, nor need be timorous.   10
But wonder at a greater wonder, for to us
Created nature doth these things subdue,
But their Creator, whom sin, nor nature tied,
For us, his creatures, and his foes, hath died.

13

What if this present were the world's last night?
Mark in my heart, O soul, where thou dost dwell,
The picture of Christ crucified, and tell
Whether that countenance can thee affright,
Tears in his eyes quench the amazing light,   5
Blood fills his frowns, which from his pierc'd head fell.
And can that tongue adjudge thee unto hell,
Which pray'd forgiveness for his foes' fierce spite?
No, no; but as in my idolatry
I said to all my profane mistresses,   10

Beauty, of pity, foulness only is
A sign of rigour: so I say to thee,
To wicked spirits are horrid shapes assign'd,
This beauteous form assures a piteous mind.

14

Batter my heart, three-person'd God; for, you
As yet but knock, breathe, shine, and seek to mend;
That I may rise, and stand, o'erthrow me, and bend
Your force, to break, blow, burn, and make me new.
I, like an usurp'd town, to another due,   5
Labour to admit you, but oh, to no end,
Reason your viceroy in me, me should defend,
But is captiv'd, and proves weak or untrue.
Yet dearly I love you, and would be loved fain,
But am betroth'd unto your enemy: 10
Divorce me, untie, or break that knot again,
Take me to you, imprison me, for I
Except you enthral me, never shall be free,
Nor ever chaste, except you ravish me.

15

Wilt thou love God, as he thee? then digest,
My soul, this wholesome meditation,
How God the Spirit, by angels waited on
In heaven, doth make his temple in thy breast.
The Father having begot a Son most blest,   5
And still begetting (for he ne'er begun),
Hath deign'd to choose thee by adoption,
Coheir to his glory, and Sabbath's endless rest;
And as a robb'd man, which by search doth find
His stol'n stuff sold, must lose or buy it again: 10
The Son of glory came down, and was slain,
Us whom he had made, and Satan stol'n, to unbind.
'Twas much, that man was made like God before,
But, that God should be made like man, much more.

17

Since she whom I lov'd hath paid her last debt
To nature, and to hers, and my good is dead,

And her soul early into heaven ravished,
Wholly on heavenly things my mind is set.
Here the admiring her my mind did whet   5
To seek thee God; so streams do show their head;
But though I have found thee, and thou my thirst hast fed,
A holy thirsty dropsy melts me yet.
But why should I beg more love, when as thou
Dost woo my soul for hers; off 'ring all thine: 10
And dost not only fear lest I allow
My love to saints and angels, things divine,
But in thy tender jealousy dost doubt
Lest the world, flesh, yea Devil put thee out.

18

Show me, dear Christ, thy spouse, so bright and clear.
What! is it she, which on the other shore
Goes richly painted? or which robb'd and tore
Laments and mourns in Germany and here?
Sleeps she a thousand, then peeps up one year?   5
Is she self truth and errs? now new, now outwore?
Doth she, and did she, and shall she evermore
On one, on seven, or on no hill appear?
Dwells she with us, or like adventuring knights
First travail we to seek and then make love?   10
Betray kind husband thy spouse to our sights,
And let mine amorous soul court thy mild dove,
Who is most true, and pleasing to thee, then
When she's embrac'd and open to most men.

19

Oh, to vex me, contraries meet in one:
Inconstancy unnaturally hath begot
A constant habit; that when I would not
I change in vows, and in devotion.
As humorous is my contrition   5
As my profane love, and as soon forgot:
As riddlingly distemper'd, cold and hot,
As praying, as mute; as infinite, as none.
I durst not view heaven yesterday; and today
In prayers, and flattering speeches I court God: 10

Tomorrow I quake with true fear of his rod.
So my devout fits come and go away
Like a fantastic ague: save that here
Those are my best days, when I shake with fear.

Upon the Annunciation and Passion

Falling upon one day. 1608

Tamely, frail body, abstain today; today
My soul eats twice, Christ hither and away.
She sees him man, so like God made in this,
That of them both a circle emblem is,
Whose first and last concur; this doubtful day   5
Of feast or fast, Christ came, and went away.
She sees him nothing twice at once, who's all;
She sees a cedar plant itself, and fall,
Her maker put to making, and the head
Of life, at once, not yet alive, yet dead.   10
She sees at once the virgin mother stay
Reclus'd at home, public at Golgotha;
Sad and rejoic'd she's seen at once, and seen
At almost fifty, and at scarce fifteen.
At once a son is promis'd her, and gone,   15
Gabriel gives Christ to her, he her to John;
Not fully a mother, she's in orbity,
At once receiver and the legacy.
All this, and all between, this day hath shown,
Th' abridgement of Christ's story, which makes one   20
(As in plain maps, the furthest west is east)
Of the angel's *Ave*, and *Consummatum est*.
How well the Church, God's court of faculties
Deals, in sometimes, and seldom joining these!
As by the self-fix'd pole we never do   25
Direct our course, but the next star thereto,
Which shows where th' other is, and which we say
(Because it strays not far) doth never stray;
So God by his Church, nearest to him, we know,
And stand firm, if we by her motion go;   30
His Spirit, as his fiery pillar doth
Lead, and his Church, as cloud; to one end both.
This Church, by letting these days join, hath shown

Death and conception in mankind is one:
Or 'twas in him the same humility,   35
That he would be a man, and leave to be:
Or as creation he hath made, as God,
With the last judgement, but one period,
His imitating spouse would join in one
Manhood's extremes: he shall come, he is gone: 40
Or as though one blood drop, which thence did fall,
Accepted, would have serv'd, he yet shed all;
So though the least of his pains, deeds, or words,
Would busy a life, she all this day affords;
This treasure then, in gross, my soul uplay,   45
And in my life retail it every day.

Good Friday, 1613. Riding Westward

Let man's soul be a sphere, and then, in this,
The intelligence that moves, devotion is,
And as the other spheres, by being grown
Subject to foreign motions, lose their own,
And being by others hurried every day,   5
Scarce in a year their natural form obey:
Pleasure or business, so, our souls admit
For their first mover, and are whirl'd by it.
Hence is 't, that I am carried towards the west
This day, when my soul's form bends towards the east.   10
There I should see a sun, by rising set,
And by that setting endless day beget;
But that Christ on this Cross, did rise and fall,
Sin had eternally benighted all.
Yet dare I almost be glad, I do not see   15
That spectacle of too much weight for me.
Who sees God's face, that is self life, must die;
What a death were it then to see God die?
It made his own lieutenant Nature shrink,
It made his footstool crack, and the sun wink.   20
Could I behold those hands which span the poles,
And turn all spheres at once, pierc'd with those holes?
Could I behold that endless height which is
Zenith to us, and our antipodes,
Humbled below us? or that blood which is   25
The seat of all our souls, if not of his,
Made dirt of dust, or that flesh which was worn,
By God, for his apparel, ragg'd, and torn?
If on these things I durst not look, durst I
Upon his miserable mother cast mine eye,   30
Who was God's partner here, and furnish'd thus
Half of that sacrifice, which ransom'd us?
Though these things, as I ride, be from mine eye,
They're present yet unto my memory,
For that looks towards them; and thou look'st towards me,   35

O Saviour, as thou hang'st upon the tree;
I turn my back to thee, but to receive
Corrections, till thy mercies bid thee leave.
O think me worth thine anger, punish me,
Burn off my rusts, and my deformity,   40
Restore thine image, so much, by thy grace,
That thou may'st know me, and I'll turn my face.

To Mr Tilman after he had taken orders

Thou, whose diviner soul hath caus'd thee now
To put thy hand unto the holy plough,
Making lay-scornings of the Ministry
Not an impediment, but victory,
What bringst thou home with thee? how is thy mind 5
Affected since the vintage? Dost thou find
New thoughts and stirrings in thee? and as steel
Touch'd with a lodestone, dost new motions feel?
Or, as a ship after much pain and care,
For iron and cloth brings home rich Indian ware, 10
Hast thou thus traffick'd, but with far more gain
Of noble goods, and with less time and pain?
Thou art the same materials, as before,
Only the stamp is changed; but no more.
And as new crown'd kings alter the face, 15
But not the money's substance, so hath grace
Chang'd only God's old image by creation,
To Christ's new stamp, at this thy coronation;
Or, as we paint angels with wings, because
They bear God's message, and proclaim his laws, 20
Since thou must do the like and so must move,
Art thou new feather'd with celestial love?
Dear, tell me where thy purchase lies, and show
What thy advantage is above, below.
But if thy gainings do surmount expression, 25
Why doth the foolish world scorn that profession,
Whose joys pass speech? Why do they think unfit
That gentry should join families with it?
As if their day were only to be spent
In dressing, mistressing and compliment; 30
Alas poor joys, but poorer men, whose trust
Seems richly placed in refined dust;
(For, such are clothes and beauty, which though gay,
Are, at the best, but as sublimed clay).
Let then the world thy calling disrespect, 35

But go thou on, and pity their neglect.
What function is so noble, as to be
Ambassador to God and destiny?
To open life, to give kingdoms to more
Than kings give dignities; to keep heaven's door?   40
Mary's prerogative was to bear Christ, so
'Tis preachers' to convey him, for they do
As angels out of clouds, from pulpits speak;
And bless the poor beneath, the lame, the weak.
If then th' astronomers, whereas they spy   45
A new-found star, their optics magnify,
How brave are those, who with their engine, can
Bring man to heaven, and heaven again to man?
These are thy titles and pre-eminences,
In whom must meet God's graces, men's offences,   50
And so the heavens which beget all things here,
And the earth our mother, which these things doth bear,
Both these in thee, are in thy calling knit,
And make thee now a blest hermaphrodite.

A Hymn to Christ

At the Author's last going into Germany

In what torn ship soever I embark,
That ship shall be my emblem of thy Ark;
What sea soever swallow me, that flood
Shall be to me an emblem of thy blood;
Though thou with clouds of anger do disguise   5
Thy face, yet through that mask I know those eyes,
   Which, though they turn away sometimes,
     They never will despise.

I sacrifice this Island unto thee,
And all whom I lov'd there, and who lov'd me;   10
When I have put our seas 'twixt them and me,
Put thou thy sea betwixt my sins and thee.
As the tree's sap doth seek the root below
In winter, in my winter now I go,
   Where none but thee, th' eternal root   15
     Of true love I may know.

Nor thou nor thy religion dost control
The amorousness of an harmonious soul,
But thou would'st have that love thyself: as thou
Art jealous, Lord, so I am jealous now,   20
Thou lov'st not, till from loving more, thou free
My soul; who ever gives, takes liberty:
   O, if thou car'st not whom I love
     Alas, thou lov'st not me.

Seal then this bill of my divorce to all,   25
On whom those fainter beams of love did fall;
Marry those loves, which in youth scattered be
On fame, wit, hopes (false mistresses), to thee.
Churches are best for prayer, that have least light:
To see God only, I go out of sight: 30
   And to 'scape stormy days, I choose
     An everlasting night.

Hymn to God my God, in my Sickness

Since I am coming to that holy room,
　Where, with thy choir of saints for evermore,
I shall be made thy music, as I come
　I tune the instrument here at the door,
　And what I must do then, think now before.　　　　5

Whilst my physicians by their love are grown
　Cosmographers, and I their map, who lie
Flat on this bed, that by them may be shown
　That this is my south-west discovery
　Per fretum febris, by these straits to die,　　　　10

I joy, that in these straits, I see my west;
　For, though their currents yield return to none,
What shall my west hurt me? As west and east
　In all flat maps (and I am one) are one,
　So death doth touch the Resurrection.　　　　15

Is the Pacific Sea my home? Or are
　The eastern riches? Is Jerusalem?
Anyan, and Magellan, and Gibraltar,
　All straits, and none but straits, are ways to them,
　Whether where Japhet dwelt, or Cham, or Shem.　　　　20

We think that Paradise and Calvary,
　Christ's Cross, and Adam's tree, stood in one place;
Look Lord, and find both Adams met in me;
　As the first Adam's sweat surrounds my face,
　May the last Adam's blood my soul embrace.　　　　25

So, in his purple wrapp'd receive me Lord,
　By these his thorns give me his other crown;
And as to others' souls I preach'd thy word,
　Be this my text, my sermon to mine own,
　Therefore that he may raise the Lord throws down.　　　　30

A Hymn to God the Father

1

Wilt thou forgive that sin where I begun,
　　Which is my sin, though it were done before?
Wilt thou forgive that sin, through which I run,
　　And do run still: though still I do deplore?
　　　When thou hast done, thou hast not done,   5
　　　　　For, I have more.

2

Wilt thou forgive that sin by which I have won
　　Others to sin? and made my sin their door?
Wilt thou forgive that sin which I did shun
　　A year, or two: but wallowed in, a score?   10
　　　When thou hast done, thou hast not done,
　　　　　For, I have more.

3

I have a sin of fear, that when I have spun
　　My last thread, I shall perish on the shore;
Swear by thyself, that at my death thy son   15
　　Shall shine as he shines now, and heretofore;
　　　And, having done that, thou hast done,
　　　　　I fear no more.

Notes

The notes are intended to explain ambiguous or obscure references (often concerning contemporary ideas or events), to clarify unfamiliar usages and sentence constructions, to point to possible interpretations of complex or condensed passages, and occasionally to indicate the circumstances of composition. They do not aim to 'paraphrase' the poems: such a procedure would defeat its purposes, proving harder to grasp than the poems themselves, and infinitely less effective and attractive.

'The Good-Morrow': l. 3 **suck'd on country pleasures, childishly:** suckled, reared, on rustic (simple, unrefined, coarse) pleasures, like children. l. 4 **seven sleepers' den:** the cave in which seven Christian youths from Ephesus, fleeing from persecution (AD 250), slept for 187 years. l. 5 **but this:** except for this. l. 10 **love all love of other sights controls:** love inhibits love of, pleasure in, other sights than the beloved. l. 13 **maps:** charts of the heavens. **other:** others. l. 18 **sharp north . . . declining west:** cold and bleak north . . . west, where the sun descends: images of fading love. l. 19 **What ever dies, was not mixt equally:** disease and death were attributed to an imbalance of elements or 'humours' in the body.

'Song (Go, and catch a falling star)': l. 2 **mandrake:** plant with forked root; supposedly, its shriek when pulled out of the ground killed whoever heard it. l. 5 **mermaids:** sirens.

'Woman's Constancy': 'The title ought to be – Mutual Inconstancy' (Coleridge). l. 14 **lunatic:** under the influence of the moon, i.e. changeable. **'scapes:** subterfuges.

'The Undertaking': l. 1 **braver:** more remarkable. l. 2 **the Worthies:** nine traditional heroes, drawn from the Old Testament, classical history and chivalric romance. l. 6 **specular stone:** ancient transparent building material, 'a thing unknown to our late times' (Donne, 'To the Countess of Bedford'). l. 22 **profane:** uninitiated, seeing love only as sexual satisfaction.

'The Sun Rising': l. 7 the King will ride: James I was a keen huntsman.
l. 8 country ants: slavish labourers. **offices:** tasks. **l. 9 all alike:** always
the same, unchanging. **l. 10 rags of time:** as compared with timeless-
ness. **l. 17 both th'Indias:** the East Indies (spice), the West Indies (gold).
l. 24 alchemy: imitation, spurious. **l. 27 asks:** requires. **l. 30 sphere:**
the sun's orbit round the earth ('centre'), according to the Ptolemaic
system.

'The Canonization': ll. 2–3 chide my palsy . . . : scold me for being too
old to throw away my fortune for love. **l. 5 Take you a course:** adopt a
course of action, a career. **place:** position (at Court). **l. 6 Observe his
Honour, or his Grace:** pay court to a lord or bishop. **l. 7 stamp'd face:**
on coins, i.e. seek wealth. **l. 8 approve:** try out. **l. 15 plaguy bill:** the list
of those dead of the plague. **l. 17 which quarrels move:** who stir up
quarrels. **l. 20 fly:** they are both the moth and the candle in whose flame it
dies. **l. 21 die:** alluding to sexual orgasm. **l. 22 the eagle and the dove:**
symbolic respectively of strength and masculinity, and of gentleness and
femininity. **l. 23 phoenix:** mythical Arabian bird, living a thousand years
and then burning itself to ashes from which the new phoenix is born; hence
literally unique. **hath more wit:** makes stronger sense. **l. 29 hearse:**
canopy over a tomb. **l. 31 chronicle:** history. **l. 32 sonnets:** love poems.
l. 33 becomes: befits. **l. 35 approve:** confirm. **l. 39 now is rage:** i.e. for
a later generation love has become rage and agitation. **l. 44 beg:** i.e. on
behalf of us later lovers.

'The Triple Fool': l. 7 purge sea-water's fretful salt: sea water was
believed to be filtered by its passage in rivers ('lanes') through the earth.
l. 10 numbers: poetic metre. **l. 14 set:** set to music.

'Lovers' Infiniteness': l. 14 in thy heart, since: i.e. since then, later.
ll. 21–2 The ground . . . have it all: i.e. crops belong to the owner of
the land on which they grow.

'Song (Sweetest love, I do not go)': said by Izaak Walton (*Life of John Donne*,
1640) to have been written for Donne's wife when he was leaving for the
Continent in 1611. **l. 8 feign'd deaths:** i.e. absences. **l. 22 our
strength:** i.e. the strength of our misery. **ll. 25–7 When thou sigh'st . . .
When thou weep'st:** sighs and tears were supposed to shorten life.
l. 33 divining: prophetic.

'A Fever': **l. 8 vapours:** evaporates. **ll. 11–12 but thy ghost, But corrupt worms:** only ... only. **ll. 13–14 wrangling schools ...:** philosophers squabbling over the nature of the fire which shall at last destroy the world. **l. 24 unchangeable firmament:** the incorruptible heavens, unlike our world and its ephemeral meteors. **l. 25 seizing:** taking possession. **l. 26 persever:** stressed on second syllable: persevere, persist.

'Air and Angels': **l. 4 affect:** also, influence. **l. 5 Still:** always. **l. 6 lovely glorious nothing:** cf. Donne elsewhere: 'If that be simply perfectest/Which can by no way be exprest/But negatives ...'; the tradition of defining God by what he is not rather than by what he is. **l. 9 subtle:** rarefied. **l. 17 admiration:** pronounced as five syllables. **l. 18 pinnace:** small light vessel. **l. 19 Every thy hair:** thy every hair. **l. 25 sphere:** the orbit of the sun around the earth (Ptolemaic). **ll. 26–8 Just such disparity ... will ever be:** a controversial point, whether the lines suggest that men's love is purer than women's or the other way about; the analogy implies that either way the difference is a fine one.

'The Anniversary': **l. 3 as they pass:** referring to 'times' and/or 'kings', 'favourites', 'glory', 'the sun itself'. **l. 11 corse:** corpse. **l. 18 inmates:** temporary residents, lodgers. **prove:** experience. **l. 19 there above:** in heaven. **l. 20 souls from their graves remove:** souls leave their bodies. **l. 22 no more, than all the rest:** because in heaven all souls are equally blessed. **l. 24 of such:** such kings. **l. 27 refrain:** refrain from, restrain. **l. 30 threescore:** i.e. diamond jubilee.

'Twickenham Garden': Twickenham Park was the residence of Lucy, Countess of Bedford, Donne's friend and patroness. **l. 1 surrounded:** overflowing. **l. 6 spider:** spiders were thought to turn everything into poison. **l.7 manna:** the food of the Israelites in the desert (Exodus 16:14–15). **l. 9 serpent:** Satan, the serpent in the Garden of Eden. **l. 16 senseless:** insensible. **l. 17 mandrake:** see note to 'Song (Go, and catch a falling star)' above. **l. 21 try:** test. **l. 26 is true:** i.e. is faithful to her present lover or husband and therefore 'kills me'.

'Love's Growth': **l. 1 pure:** unmixed, therefore not subject to change. **ll. 7–8 cures all sorrow/With more:** cf. homoeopathic medicine or mithridatic treatment. **l. 11 use:** are accustomed. **l. 13 elemented:** compounded of different elements; love is a mixture of mind ('sometimes would contemplate') and body ('sometimes do'). **l. 15 eminent:** conspicuous. **l. 23 spheres:** in which the planets were thought to be carried, 'concentric' to the earth. **l. 26 times of action:** e.g. of war or emergency.

'The Dream': **l. 7 so truth:** such truth, essentially truth. **l. 16 beyond an angel's art:** because one's thoughts are known only to God. **l. 21 show'd thee, thee:** showed you to be yourself. **l. 22 doubt:** suspect. **l. 25 pure, and brave:** unalloyed and confident. **l. 28 Men light and put out:** cf. 'A torch that hath been lighted, and used before, is easier lighted than a new torch' (Donne in a sermon).

'A Valediction: Of Weeping': **l. 3 coins:** gives value to. **l. 8 that thou:** that image of you. **l. 9 on a diverse shore:** in different countries, separated by a sea (the 'tear' that 'falls'). **l. 10 round ball:** globe. **l. 13 nothing:** merely an O, a blank ball. **l. 27 Whoe'er sighs most . . . :** see note to 'When thou sigh'st' in 'Song (Sweetest love, I do not go)', above.

'Love's Alchemy': **l. 2 centric:** central, essential. **l. 3 told:** counted. **l. 7 chemic:** alchemist. **th'elixir:** the elixir of life, supposed to heal all diseases and prolong life. **l. 8 pregnant pot:** alchemist's crucible, compared to a womb during pregnancy. **l. 9 If by the way:** i.e. though he hasn't discovered the elixir, the alchemist will be happy to find some perfume or medical cure during his search. **l. 12 winter-seeming:** cold and short. **l. 15 my man:** my servant. **l. 17 short scorn:** brief humiliation. **play:** role. **l. 22 that day's rude hoarse minstrelsy:** the wedding day's crude and noisy celebrations. **spheres:** i.e. the music of the spheres; cf. 'There's not the smallest orb . . . But in his motion like an angel sings' (Shakespeare, *Merchant of Venice*). **l. 24 mummy:** body without mind. **possest:** held in absolute mastery; enjoyed sexually; possessed by a demon.

'The Flea': 'Ribald love poems on fleas proliferated in the sixteenth century . . . The poet commonly envied the flea's free access to his mistress's body, or its death by her hand at the climax of its bliss' (A.J. Smith, *John Donne: The Complete English Poems*, 1971). **l. 16 use:** habit.

'The Curse': a long-established subject for verse: 'A certain ancient form of poesy by which men did use to reproach their enemies' (George Puttenham, 1589). **l. 3 His only, and only his purse:** his only purse, and only his purse. **l. 8 fear of missing . . . getting, torn:** torn between the fear of not winning her and the shame of winning her. **l. 12 fame:** public opinion, i.e. may he be concerned only for scandal. **l. 14 scarceness:** poverty. **l. 16 incestuously an heir begot:** i.e. disinherited himself by fathering an heir on a kinswoman who otherwise would have left her estate to him. **l. 22 parasites:** hangers-on. **l. 23 fain be theirs:** gladly be a parasite on those parasites. **l. 24 circumcis'd for bread:** become a Jew in order to share the community's charity or ritual feasting. **l. 26 interwish:** wish each other. **l. 30 schedules:** supplements, codicils. **l. 32 out-cursed:** nature has already made her 'curst', i.e. a shrew.

'*The Message*': **l. 4 forc'd:** affected, artificial. **l. 14 cross:** break. **l. 23 will none:** will have nothing to do with you.

'*A Nocturnal upon St Lucy's Day*': 13 December, formerly the shortest day of the year, and the festival of St Lucy, patron saint of light, associated with it by her name (*lux*: light); Lucy was the name of Donne's patroness, the Countess of Bedford. **l. 3 flasks:** gunpowder-horns. **l. 4 light squibs:** light charges of gunpowder, i.e. weak emissions of sunlight. **l. 6 general balm:** the essence of life. **hydroptic:** dropsical, thirsty in the extreme. **l. 7 to the bed's-feet:** it was believed that in dying men life ebbed away from the feet. **l. 13 new alchemy:** new because love extracts a quintessence from 'nothingness'. **l. 14 express:** extract. **l. 21 limbeck:** alembic, retort used in alchemical distillation. **l. 29 the first nothing:** the 'nothing' from which God created the world. **l. 34 invest:** are endued with. **l. 37 my sun:** his dead lover. **l. 38 lesser sun:** the real sun. **l. 39 Goat:** the sign of the Goat (Capricorn); also, goats were traditionally associated with lust (Pan).

'*Witchcraft by a Picture*': **l.6 made and marr'd:** witches were said to kill their victims by making and then destroying pictures of them.

'*The Bait*': Izaak Walton claimed that the poem was intended to show that Donne could write mellifluously when he wanted to; it is a sequel to Marlowe's 'The Passionate Shepherd to his Love' ('Come live with me, and be my love') and Ralegh's 'The Nymph's Reply'. **l. 8 Begging:** begging that. **l. 17 reeds:** rods. **l. 20 windowy:** because of its 'windows' or meshes. **l. 23 curious:** artful. **sleave-silk flies:** lures made from unravelled silk threads.

'*The Apparition*': **l. 3 solicitation:** pronounced as six syllables. **l. 5**

feign'd vestal: pretendedly chaste. **l. 6 wink:** flicker, as about to go out. **l. 11 aspen:** trembling. **l. 13 verier:** truer. **l. 17 Than ... rest still innocent:** than be dissuaded by my threats and remain innocent.

'The Broken Heart': **l. 4 ten:** i.e. ten victims. **l. 8 flask of powder:** gunpowder-horn. **l. 14 chaws:** chews. **l. 15 chain'd shot:** cannon balls chained together so as to mow down whole ranks of the enemy. **l. 16 fry:** young, small fish. **ll. 25–6 nothing can ... be empty quite:** no matter can be totally annihilated, nor can there be an absolute vacuum. **l. 29 broken glasses:** broken mirrors.

'A Valediction: Forbidding Mourning': **l. 6 tear-floods ... sigh-tempests:** the stock-in-trade of Petrarchan love poets. **move:** stir up. **l. 8 laity:** the uninitiated ('dull', 'sublunary'). **l. 9 Moving of th'earth:** earthquakes, thought to portend some evil. **l. 11 trepidation:** oscillation (actually due to the slight wobble of the earth on its axis). **l. 12 innocent:** harmless. **l. 13 sublunary:** earthly, hence inferior. **l. 14 sense:** dependent on the senses ('eyes, lips, and hands'). **admit:** allow, bear. **l. 22 endure not yet:** yet do not suffer. **l. 23 expansion:** pronounced as four syllables. **l. 24 thinness beat:** like gold leaf. **l. 26 twin compasses:** i.e. the two legs of a compass. **l. 34 obliquely run:** follow a curved path.

'The Ecstasy': **l. 5 cemented:** pronounced with stress on first and third syllables. **l. 6 fast balm:** a moisture that preserves and keeps them steadfast. **l. 11 pictures:** reflections. **get:** beget. **l. 12 propagation:** pronounced as five syllables. **l. 27 concoction:** in alchemical sense, purification. **l. 30 what we love:** the nature of our love. **l. 33 several:** separate. **l. 36 each this and that:** the united soul contains two souls, his and hers. **l. 42 Interinanimates:** in some versions 'Interanimates'. **l. 44 Defects of loneliness:** defects due to singleness ('controlled' by the 'abler' joint soul). **l. 47 atomies:** atoms, components. **l. 52 intelligences:** spirits governing the celestial spheres. **l. 56 dross ... allay:** impurity ... alloy. **ll. 57–8 heaven's influence ... imprints the air:** the stars (here, possibly angels) were thought to exert their influence on men by first influencing the air (in the case of angels, clothing themselves in air). **l. 60 repair:** go. **ll. 61–2 blood ... Spirits:** the vapours ('spirits') linking soul to body were held to come from the blood. **l. 66 affections ... faculties:** feelings ... physical powers. **l. 68 prince:** love. **l. 76 Small change ... to bodies gone:** the observer will see little difference when the souls have returned to the bodies.

'**Love's Deity**': l. **5 produc'd a destiny:** ordained a fate (i.e. to love unrequitedly). l. **6 vice-nature:** substitute for nature. l. **9 young godhead:** Cupid's beginnings as a god. l. **10 even:** equal. l. **12 Actives to passives:** e.g. males to females. l. **18 purlieu:** sphere of authority. l. **22 Rebel and atheist:** rebel against 'destiny', atheist in not believing in Cupid. l. **26 loves before:** has a husband or lover already.

'**The Will**': l. **3 Argus:** in Greek mythology, a giant with a hundred eyes. l. **5 fame:** rumour, depicted as having many mouths. l. **10 planets:** etymologically 'wanderers', therefore inconstant. l. **12 ingenuity:** ingenuousness, candour. l. **13 Jesuits:** regarded as given to dissimulation and casuistry. l. **15 Capuchin:** Franciscan monk, vowed to poverty. ll. **20–1 schismatics Of Amsterdam:** extreme Protestants, believing in salvation through faith alone, and not through good works. l. **22 courtship:** courtesy. l. **23 bare:** lacking in it (modesty). l. **26 disparity:** beneath her. l. **30 schoolmen:** medieval philosophers, given to hairsplitting. l. **31 excess:** intemperance. l. **32 To Nature ... rhyme:** perhaps, because Nature stands in need of Art ('rhyme'). l. **38 physic:** medical. l. **39 Bedlam:** the lunatic asylum of St Mary of Bethlehem in London. l. **40 brazen medals:** old bronze coins having no current value. l. **45 disproportion:** make inappropriate. l. **54 all three:** the poet, his mistress, and Love.

'**The Funeral**': l. **3 subtle:** not readily understood. l. **8 dissolution:** pronounced as five syllables. l. **9 sinewy thread:** the nervous system. l. **14 except:** unless. l. **21 humility:** modesty. l. **22 To afford to it all that a soul can do:** to credit the 'wreath of hair' with all the powers of a soul (as in the first stanza). l. **23 bravery:** bravado, defiance.

'**The Blossom**': l. **12 forbidden or forbidding:** forbidden because the affair is illicit; forbidding because she repels his advances. ll. **15–16 that sun ... this sun:** the lady ... the real sun. l. **18 subtle:** ingenious. l. **31 some other part:** i.e. a sexual innuendo. l. **35 fat:** prosperous.

'**The Relic**': l. **1 broke up again:** old graves were dug up to make room for new coffins. l. **3 woman-head:** womanly nature, woman's trick. l. **6 bright:** fair. l. **10 last busy day:** the Resurrection. l. **13 misdevotion:** idolatry. l. **17 Mary Magdalene:** Christ's devoted follower; see note to 'To the Lady Magdalen Herbert', below. l. **18 A something else:** by implication Christ, or possibly one of Mary Magdalene's lovers in her unregenerate days. **l. 21 this paper:** this poem. **l. 24 what we lov'd:** what in each other we loved. **l. 27 Coming and going:** on meeting and on parting. **l. 29 seals:** restrictions. **l. 30 injur'd by late law:** nature allows love freely to all, law restricts it to marriage. **l. 32 pass:** surpass, exceed.

'The Prohibition': **l. 1 Take heed of:** beware of. **ll. 3–4 repair . . . upon:** made good by drawing upon. **l. 11 officer:** agent, instrument (of revenge). **l. 13 style:** title. **l. 18 neither's office do:** cancel out each other's effect. **l. 19 gentler way:** i.e. in sexual orgasm. **l. 22 stage:** i.e. living and lasting exhibition of her power; dead, he would merely be her 'triumph', not to be repeated.

'The Expiration': **l. 2 vapours:** evaporates. **l. 4 benight:** darken. **l. 11 Except:** unless.

'The Computation': **l. 1 since yesterday:** 'The poem's years add up to 2,400: 100 for each hour since he saw her' (John Carey, *John Donne*, 1990). **l. 4 thou would'st, they might last:** the lady would continue her favours.

'Elegy 5: His Picture': **l. 1 picture:** miniature portrait. **l. 3 dead:** absent. **l. 4 shadows both:** the picture and the poet. **l. 7 haircloth:** (like a) shirt made of hair worn by penitents. **l. 10 powder's:** gunpowder's. **l. 14 reach:** affect. **l. 19 nurse:** nourish. **l. 20 disus'd:** unaccustomed.

'Elegy 9: The Autumnal': **l. 7 Were her first years:** her first years were. **Golden Age:** legendary age of innocence and peace. **l. 8 tried:** tested. **l. 10 tolerable:** temperate. **l. 11 who asks:** he who asks. **l. 16 anachorit:** anchorite, hermit. **l. 18 a grave . . . a tomb:** a grave buries and hides; a tomb commemorates. **l. 20 progress:** a monarch's formal journey through his domain. **standing house:** fixed abode. **l. 25 underwood:** (inflammable) brushwood. **l. 27 seasonabliest:** most seasonably, opportunely. **l. 29 platane tree:** according to Herodotus, the Persian king, Xerxes, passionately admired a tall and beautiful (though barren) plane-tree he had found in Lydia. **l. 38 unthrift's:** spendthrift's. **l. 41 several:** different. **l. 42 at Resurrection:** when all the body's parts are assembled together and joined with the soul. **l. 43 death's-heads:** skulls as reminders of mortality. **l. 47 lation:** motion.

'Elegy 10: The Dream': **l. 1 Image:** mental picture. **more than she:**

more truly her than is her actual self. **l. 3 medal:** medallion. **l. 4 stamps:**
impressions. **ll. 7–8 sense . . . dull:** strong or bright objects dull our sense.
l. 8 the more, the less we see: the stronger, the less distinctly we see the
object. **l. 11 meaner:** more moderate. **l. 12 Convenient:** fitting. **l. 14
fantastical:** produced by fantasy. **l. 15 true:** real. **l. 17 a such:** such
a. **l. 19 sonnets:** love poems. **l. 24 snuff:** burnt-out wick of a candle.
l. 26 idiot: insensible.

'Elegy 16: On his Mistress': in two manuscript versions this poem is
entitled 'On his Mistress' desire to be disguised and to go like a Page with
him' and 'His wife would have gone as his Page'. **l. 1 strange:** when they
were still strangers. **interview:** meeting. **l. 3 remorse:** pity. **l. 8 want
and divorcement:** lack (of each other) and separation. **l. 14 feign'd:**
pretended. **l. 19 move:** take away. **l. 21 Boreas:** the north wind.
l. 23 Orithea: in mythology a daughter of the king of Athens whom the
rough Boreas loved; in Plato she was killed when he blew her over a cliff.
l. 24 prov'd: undergone (unnecessary dangers). **l. 27 Dissemble:**
pretend to be. **l. 34 Spitals:** hospitals, especially for venereal diseases.
l. 36 players: actors. **l. 37 know:** recognize; also 'know' in the carnal
sense. **l. 38 indifferent:** not caring whether he makes love to a woman or
a man. **l. 41 Lot's fair guests:** the two angels, assumed to be men, whom
the Sodomites demanded of Lot, 'that we may know them' (Genesis 19:
1–5). **l. 42 spongy hydroptic:** soaked in drink. **l. 44 only a worthy
gallery:** the only worthy gallery (antechamber). **l. 46 greatest King:**
God; conceivably Love. **l. 55 Augur:** predict (a better fate for me). **except:**
unless.

'Elegy 19: To his Mistress Going to Bed': l. 1 all rest my powers defy:
his virile powers prevent rest or inaction. **l. 2 in labour:** in impatient
anticipation. **l. 4 standing:** waiting; pun on erection. **l. 5 heaven's
zone:** the Milky Way. **l. 7 breastplate:** (jewelled) stomacher. **l. 9 chime:**
of her watch; or possibly the sound of 'unlacing'. **l. 11 busk:** corset.
l. 12 still can be: can remain still, unmoved (though so close).
l. 15 coronet: head-dress. **l. 21 Mahomet's paradise:** i.e. rich in beauti-
ful houris. **l. 23 these angels:** women. **l. 24 Those set our hairs, but
these our flesh upright:** evil spirits make our hair stand on end in terror,
women excite us sexually. **l. 29 empery:** empire. **l. 30 discovering:**
also, uncovering. **l. 31 bonds:** commitments; also her arms. **l. 32 seal:**
symbol of possession; cf. 'Set me as a seal upon thy heart' (Song of Solomon
8:6). **l. 36 Atlanta's balls:** in the legend the suitor Hippomenes won

Atalanta's hand by beating her in a race: at intervals he dropped three golden balls which she stopped to pick up; here the roles are reversed. **l. 40 laymen:** outsiders, as opposed to 'only we' below. **l. 42 imputed grace:** divine grace bestowed in order to lead others to salvation. **l. 46 penance . . . innocence:** both represented by the colour white; two versions have the milder line, 'There is no penance due to innocence'. **l. 48 more covering:** more clothes; also, a man is sufficient covering.

'An Epithalamion, or Marriage Song': **Epithalamion:** epithalamium, song celebrating a marriage. Princess Elizabeth, daughter of James I, was married to Frederick, Elector Palatine, on 14 February 1613. **l. 1 Bishop Valentine:** the saint, whose feast-day is 14 February, had jurisdiction ('diocese') over flying things; cf. 'Saint Valentine's Day,/When ev'ry fowl cometh there to choose his mate' (Chaucer). **l. 7 sparrow:** whose short life was attributed to its lechery. **l. 8 stomacher:** waistcoat; i.e. the robin. **l. 9 speed:** prosper (even though black was considered an ill-favoured colour). **l. 10 halcyon:** kingfisher. **l. 11 sped:** matched. **l. 14 inflame:** excite. **l. 18 two phoenixes:** impossible, since only one phoenix could exist at any one time; see note to 'The Canonization' above. **l. 20 the Ark:** being legendary, the phoenix would find no place in Noah's Ark. **l. 27 courage:** sexual vitality. **l. 37 blazing:** comets were believed to portend the deaths of kings and princes. **l. 40 Ends:** purposes. **l. 42 date records:** as events are dated from the appearance of the star at Christ's nativity. **l. 52 his way:** by marriage ('this Bishop's knot'). **divers:** various. **l. 55 one way left:** sexual consummation. **l. 67 masquers:** those performing the marriage entertainment. **l. 75 nicely:** meticulously (thus wasting more time). **l. 90 coin:** love-making. **l. 94 acquittances:** acknowledgements of debts paid. **l. 98 turtles:** turtle-doves. **l. 104 satyrs:** i.e. revelling till dawn. **l. 105 let out day:** day breaks when their eyes open and light the world. **l. 108 which side:** i.e. of the curtained bed. **l. 111 tried:** tested. **l. 112 enlarge:** prolong.

'Epithalamion made at Lincoln's Inn': **l. 4 print:** impression. **l. 5 dint:** indent. **l. 12 put on . . . a woman's name:** become truly and completely a woman. **l. 14 furnish'd:** well supplied. **l. 16 Thousands of angels:** i.e. of English gold coins (as dowry). **l. 17 device:** inventiveness. **l. 19 Conceitedly:** fancifully. **l. 22 Flora:** Roman goddess of flowers. **Ind:** India, reputedly opulent. **l. 23 in nothing lame:** deficient in nothing (including her virginity). **l. 25 frolic:** merry. **l. 27 painted:** showy. **l. 28 but your beasts love none:** love nothing but your cattle.

l. **29 fellowships:** the Inns of Court, the legal societies. l. **30 hermaphrodites:** combining opposites, i.e. 'study and play'. l. **34 Except:** unless. l. **37 two-leav'd:** double. l. **41 Long time:** a long time after. l. **43 elder claims:** prior claims on the love of either partner. l. **50 for they:** because they. l. **56 shadows turn:** after the hour of noon they turn in the opposite direction. l. **57 nill:** will not. l. **61 evening star:** Venus. l. **62 our amorous star:** the bride. l. **64 truce:** respite. l. **67 toil'd:** hard-worked. l. **68 dispens'd:** dispensed with. l. **71 turn:** return. ll. **81–2 but able To be:** only potentially. l. **86 spent:** exchanged. l. **87 style:** title, status. l. **90 embowel:** disembowel, as in the sacrifice of a paschal lamb. l. **91 watch:** stay awake. l. **93 This sun:** the bride. l. **94 want:** lack. l. **95 Wonders are wrought:** i.e. what had no fault before now becomes perfect. **maim:** deficiency or imperfection; see note on 'in nothing lame' above.

'Satire 3': in one MS entitled 'Of Religion'. l. **1 Kind pity:** fellow-feeling. **spleen:** considered the seat of both melancholy and mirth. l. **3 be wise:** follow the wise course and neither laugh at sins nor weep over them. l. **4 worn:** ingrained. l. **7 blinded age:** the pagan, pre-Christian era, which lacked the light of revealed truth (but respected virtue and honour). l. **8 valiant:** powerful. l. **9 to them:** to the pagans. l. **10 means:** i.e. the enlightenment of Christianity. l. **12 blind:** as 'blinded age' above. l. **13 may be imputed:** a cautious suggestion that a virtuous life might compensate for the absence of Christian faith. l. **14 near:** direct. l. **17 mutinous Dutch:** who had attempted to free themselves from their Spanish overlords since 1572. l. **22 north discoveries:** expeditions to discover a north-west passage to the east round the north of the American continent. l. **23 salamanders:** lizards popularly regarded as cold-blooded and able to live in fire. ll. **23–4 divine Children:** the three men saved by God when Nebuchadnezzar cast them into a fiery furnace (Daniel 3). l. **24 fires of Spain:** *autos-da-fé* of the Spanish Inquisition. **line:** equator. l. **25 limbecks:** alembics. l. **26 for gain bear:** endure (these hardships) for monetary gain. l. **27 draw:** draw his sword. l. **30 thy foes and his:** your foes and God's. l. **32 forbidden wars:** wars fought for worldly reasons (contrasted with 'th'appointed field', where Christians fight in God's name). l. **35 fain:** gladly. **to be quit:** in return. l. **38 wane:** decline. l. **43 Mirreus:** i.e. a Catholic. l. **47 rags:** remnants of truth. l. **48 statecloth:** canopy over the monarch's throne. l. **49 Crants:** i.e. a Calvinist. **brave:** showy. l. **50 Geneva:** home of Calvinism, a doctrine emphasizing predestination and justification by faith alone. l. **51 sullen:**

dismal. **l. 53 humours:** dispositions. **l. 55 Graius:** i.e. an Anglican. **l. 58 is only perfect:** is alone perfect. **l. 60 Tender to him:** offer to him. **being tender:** young and weak. **l. 62 values:** fines imposed on wards who refused a marriage proposed by their guardians. **Phrygius:** i.e. a nonconformist. **l. 65 Gracchus:** i.e. a liberal or latitudinarian. **l. 66 divers:** different. **l. 67 habits:** costumes. **ll. 68–9 this blindness too much light breeds:** too much 'enlightenment' or broad-mindedness leads to blindness (to the truth). **l. 69 unmoved:** uninfluenced by other factors. **l. 70 Of force:** of necessity. **forc'd:** when compelled to choose. **l. 71 ask thy father:** cf. 'Remember the days of old . . . ask thy father, and he will show thee; thy elders, and they will tell thee' (Deuteronomy 32:7). **l. 75 not of none, nor worst:** not of no faith, nor of the worst faith. **l. 76 adore, or scorn:** worship like Catholics, spurn like anti-Catholics. **protest:** like Protestants. **l. 79 sleep:** do nothing. **run wrong:** take the wrong path. **l. 81 about . . . and about:** round about, gradually making one's way upwards. **l. 82 suddenness:** steepness, abruptness. **l. 84 none can work:** cf. 'the night cometh, when no man can work' (John 9:4). **l. 85 To will:** to intend in the future, as opposed to 'now do'. **l. 86 Hard deeds, the body's pains:** through the body's pains hard deeds are achieved ('reached'). **l. 90 so ill case:** such an evil condition. **l. 91 Sign'd . . . blank-charters:** given a free hand. **l. 92 vicars:** agents of God. **hangmen to:** executors of orders from. **l. 95 last day:** Judgement Day. **boot:** profit. **ll. 96–7 Philip . . . Gregory . . . Harry . . . Martin:** the Catholic Philip of Spain . . . Pope Gregory . . . the Protestant Henry VIII of England . . . Luther. **l. 98 mere:** absolute. **l. 109 more choose:** rather choose.

'To Sir Henry Wotton': Wotton was a lawyer, courtier, diplomat, poet, and close friend of Donne. **l. 2 Cadiz' or Saint Michael's tale:** referring to the expeditions against Cadiz (1596) and the Azores (1597); Donne and Wotton had taken part in both, hence it would be no 'news' to either of them. **l. 4 stomachs:** appetites. **l. 5 may God frown:** an oath adding emphasis to what he is saying. **l. 11 commissary:** deputy. **throughly:** thoroughly. **l. 12 squadron:** continuing the 'warfare' metaphor. **marshal their state:** (condemn to) follow their calling at Court. **l. 13 silly:** simple, innocent. **l. 14 wishing prayers:** i.e. asking for their rights. **neat:** pure. **l. 15 Like Indian . . . they be:** referring to the innocent and unarmed South American Indians massacred by the conquistadors. **l. 18 Tender to know:** sensitive to wrongs committed against oneself. **tough to acknowledge:** slow to admit to wrongs one has committed

against others. **l. 22 mimic antics:** grotesque actors. **l. 23 projects:** plots. **egregious gests:** ostentatious acts. **l. 24 morals of a game at chests:** the game of chess ('chests') was regarded as a moral allegory of power-seeking. **l. 27 At Court ... From Court ... the better style:** written at the Court, though it would be better to designate oneself as far away from the Court.

'To Mr I.L.': Mr I.L.'s identity is unknown. **l. 4 Sequan:** the river Seine. **Danuby:** the river Danube. **l. 6 Trent:** river in the north-east of England. **Lethe:** the river of forgetfulness in Hades. **l. 9 stretch'd:** extensive. **labour'd:** much worked on. **l. 13 both we:** both Mr I.L.'s friends and his Muse.

'To the Countess of Bedford': Countess of Bedford: see note to 'Twickenham Garden' above. **l. 1 sublime:** purified. **perfection:** pronounced as four syllables. **l. 3 himself had none:** since there was no one to honour him. **l. 4 of the elements, these:** earth and water. **l. 6 those are barren:** air and fire, in which nothing grows. **l. 9 but direct our honour, not bestow:** only indicate whom we should honour, not bestow honour directly. **l. 11 gross:** dross. **stilling:** distillation. **l. 12 dung:** i.e. by heating in horse-dung. **l. 15** *Te Deums:* hymns of praise. **l. 18 Sicil:** Sicily, i.e. the volcanic Mount Etna. **l. 19 darker:** in greater obscurity. **l. 21 But one:** except for God. **l. 24 last day:** the Resurrection. **l. 26 discovers:** uncovers, reveals. **quick:** lively. **l. 27 through-shine front:** transparent countenance. **l. 29 specular stone:** see note to 'The Undertaking' above. **l. 33 know and dare:** to know what is good and dare to do it. **l. 34 our souls:** plants were said to have the 'soul' of growth, and animals the 'soul' of sense; man has both and also, later in development, the 'soul' of reason. **l. 38 keep none:** remain unaffected by it ('zeal'). **l. 42 her yea, is not her no:** i.e. discretion and religion are in accord. **l. 44 break them:** by setting discretion above religion or vice versa. **wit:** intelligence (which must be an essential part of religion, not a mere 'colleague' or assistant). **l. 46 types:** emblems. **round circles:** symbolizing perfection. **l. 47 pieceless centres:** the centre of a circle, though one and indivisible, is a part of every radius. **l. 51 your ways discretion:** discretion wrought your means. **l. 54 Neither:** neither coveting (envy) nor repentance of past sins. **great and innocent:** two qualities rarely found together.

'To the Lady Magdalen Herbert': Magdalen Herbert was the mother of the poet George Herbert and a good friend to Donne and his wife. **l. 2 Bethina**

... **Magdalo:** Mary Magdalene, sister of Lazarus of Bethany, was the 'sinner' who anointed Jesus with ointment (Luke 7:37); tradition associated her with Magdala in Galilee. **jointure:** joint ownership. **ll. 4–5 knew ... The Resurrection:** she was among the first to witness Christ's rising (John 20:13–18). **l. 6 some Fathers:** some fathers of the Church held that the actions and events reported of her were to be attributed to more than one woman. **l. 12 The latter half:** the devout part of Mary Magdalene's life, as distinct from the sinner's. **l. 13 a guest:** Christ was a guest in the house of Lazarus and Mary Magdalene in Bethany: 'There they made him a supper' (John 12:1–3). **l. 14 these hymns:** which Donne enclosed with this poem, possibly the seven sonnets in the sequence 'La Corona'.

'Holy Sonnets: 1': **l. 8 weigh:** carry. **l. 11 foe:** Satan. **tempteth:** i.e. to despair. **l. 13 prevent:** frustrate. **l. 14 adamant:** a magnet.

'Holy Sonnets: 3': **l. 1 sighs and tears:** see first note to 'A Valediction: Forbidding Mourning' above. **l. 5 idolatry:** profane love, worship of women. **l. 6 rent:** rend, tear apart. **l. 7 sufferance:** suffering, also tolerance of 'idolatry'. **l. 9 hydroptic:** insatiably thirsty. **night-scouting:** prowling at night. **l. 10 self-tickling proud:** proud, self-indulgent man.

'Holy Sonnets: 4': **l. 4 turn:** return. **l. 5 death's doom:** the death sentence. **l. 7 damn'd:** condemned. **hal'd:** dragged. **execution:** pronounced as five syllables.

'Holy Sonnets: 5': **l. 1 little world:** man as a microcosm, 'an abridgement of all the world', as Donne put it elsewhere. **l. 2 elements:** matter, the traditional four elements: earth, water, air, fire. **sprite:** spirit. **ll. 5–6 You which ... Have found new spheres:** the astronomers. **l. 6 of new lands can write:** the discoverers of new countries. **l. 9 drown'd no more:** as God promised Noah after the Flood (Genesis 9:11). **l. 10 it must be burnt:** the universal conflagration 'against the day of judgement' (2 Peter 3:7). **ll. 13–14 zeal ... eating:** cf. 'the zeal of thine house hath eaten me up' (Psalm 69:9).

'Holy Sonnets: 6': **l. 3 Idly:** both lazily and foolishly. **l. 7 ever-waking part:** the immortal soul. **that face:** God's. **l. 8 Whose fear:** fear of which. **l. 13 Impute:** it is through Christ's righteousness 'imputed' to it that the soul is saved.

'Holy Sonnets: 7': l. 1 **corners:** cf. 'I saw four angels standing on the four corners of the earth' (Revelation 7:1). l. 4 **to your scatter'd bodies go:** see note to 'at Resurrection' in 'Elegy 9: The Autumnal' above. l. 5 **fire:** see note to 'it must be burnt' in 'Holy Sonnets: 5' above. ll. 7–8 **you whose eyes . . . death's woe:** those alive on the Day of Judgement; cf. 'We shall not all sleep, but we shall all be changed' (1 Corinthians 15:51).

'Holy Sonnets: 9': l. 1 **that tree:** the Tree of Knowledge in Eden (Genesis 2:17). l. 3 **serpents envious:** Satan, envious of the happiness of Adam and Eve, took the form of a serpent. l. 4 **Cannot be damn'd:** because animals lack the power of reasoned choice. l. 10 **only worthy:** alone worthy. l. 11 **Lethean:** from Lethe, the river of forgetfulness in Hades; here, 'heavenly'. l. 13 **remember them, some claim as debt:** some believe that God remembers sins, and forgives them as part of the general debt discharged by Christ's sacrifice. l. 14 **forget:** cf. 'I will forgive their iniquity, and I will remember their sin no more' (Jeremiah 31:34).

'Holy Sonnets: 10': l. 5 **but thy pictures:** mere images of you. l. 7 **soonest our best men . . . do go:** cf. 'As virtuous men pass mildly away,/And whisper to their souls,/to go' ('A Valediction: Forbidding Mourning'). l. 11 **poppy:** opium as a narcotic. **charms:** magical spells with the power to bring sleep. l. 12 **swell'st:** i.e. with pride. l. 14 **thou shalt die:** cf. 'The last enemy that shall be destroyed is death' (1 Corinthians 15:26).

'Holy Sonnets: 12': l. 1 **waited on:** served. l. 2 **prodigal:** wasteful. l. 4 **Simple:** unadulterated, more of a piece. **corruption:** pronounced as four syllables; as also **subjection** below. l. 5 **brook'st:** tolerate. l. 6 **sillily:** naïvely, meekly. l. 7 **Dissemble:** pretend. **one man's stroke:** the slaughterer's. l. 12 **these things:** the animals mentioned. l. 13 **tied:** constrained.

'Holy Sonnets: 13': l. 3 **picture of Christ crucified:** crucifix. l. 5 **amazing:** overwhelming, terrifying. l. 8 **spite:** malice. l. 9 **idolatry:** worship of false gods ('my profane mistresses'). l. 11 **only is:** is only. l. 12 **rigour:** harshness. **to thee:** to his soul. l. 14 **assures:** assures us of.

'Holy Sonnets: 14': l. 1 **three-person'd:** the Trinity: the Father, the Son, the Holy Spirit. l. 5 **to another due:** owing duty to someone other than the (usurping) power presently occupying the town. l. 9 **fain:** dearly.

l. 13 Except: unless. **enthral:** enslave. **l. 14 ravish:** take by force; as it were, rape.

'Holy Sonnets: 15': **l. 1 digest:** understand and assimilate. **l. 4 his temple in thy breast:** cf. 'Know ye not that ye are the temple of God, and that the Spirit of God dwelleth in you?' (1 Corinthians 3:16). **l. 6 still begetting:** God is outside time and begets Christ eternally. **l. 7 adoption:** pronounced as four syllables. **l. 11 Son of glory:** also, sun. **l. 12 Satan stol'n:** whom Satan had stolen. **l. 13 made like God:** cf. 'And God said, Let us make man in our image, after our likeness' (Genesis 1:26).

'Holy Sonnets: 17': **l. 1 she whom I lov'd:** Donne's wife, Ann, died on 15 August 1617, at the age of thirty-three. **l. 2 to hers:** her own mortal nature. **l. 3 ravished:** carried off (by force). **l. 6 head:** source. **l. 8 dropsy:** unsatisfied thirst. **l. 9 when as:** considering that. **l. 10 woo my soul for hers:** woo his soul on behalf of hers, now in heaven. **all thine:** all your (God's) love. **l. 13 jealousy:** zeal. **doubt:** fear. **l. 14 put thee out:** shut you out.

'Holy Sonnets: 18': cf. 'Satire 3: Kind pity chokes my spleen' above on the search for the true religion. **l. 1 thy spouse:** the (true) Church. **ll. 2–3 other shore ... richly painted:** continental Europe ... the Catholic Church. **l. 4 in Germany and here:** the Protestant Church, including Lutheranism. **l. 5 Sleeps she a thousand:** for a thousand years before the Protestant Reformation. **l. 6 self truth:** truth itself, infallible. **now new, now outwore:** e.g. like fashions in clothes. **l. 8 On one, on seven, or on no hill:** referring to Mount Moriah (on which Solomon built his temple to the Lord), Catholic Rome, and Calvinist Geneva. **l. 10 travail:** labour, also travel. **l. 11 Betray:** reveal. **l. 12 dove:** the Church as the beloved of Christ. **l. 14 embrac'd:** embraced by (continuing the 'profane' metaphor of 'make love', 'Betray ... thy spouse to our sights' and 'mine amorous soul').

'Holy Sonnets: 19': **l. 1 vex:** trouble. **l. 4 devotion:** pronounced as four syllables, as also **contrition**. **l. 5 humorous:** pertaining to the disposition: here, changeable. **l. 7 riddlingly distemper'd:** inexplicably disordered, unbalanced. **l. 8 as infinite, as none:** his contrition is now infinite, now non-existent. **l. 13 ague:** sporadic fever accompanied by fits of shaking.

'Upon the Annunciation and Passion': in 1608 the Annunciation coincided with Good Friday. **l. 1 Tamely:** submissively. **l. 2 eats twice:** because this is a double festival. **hither and away:** referring to Christ's impending birth (the Annunciation) and his death (the Passion). **l. 3 She:** his soul. **l. 4 circle:** emblem of perfection. **l. 5 doubtful:** whether feast or fast. **l. 7 nothing twice:** before his birth and after his death. **l. 8 cedar:** representing Christ; possibly alluding to the twig of cedar which God planted on a high mountain (Ezekiel 17:22–4). **l. 9 put to making:** submitted to being made. **l. 10 at once:** at the same time. **l. 12 Reclus'd:** secluded. **Golgotha:** Calvary, where Jesus was crucified. **l. 14 fifty . . . fifteen:** the Virgin's age when Jesus was crucified and when he was born. **l. 16 Gabriel:** the angel of the Annunciation (Luke 1:26–8). **he her to John:** on the Cross, 'When Jesus therefore saw his mother, and the disciple standing by, whom he loved, he saith unto his mother, Woman, behold thy son! Then saith he to the disciple, Behold thy mother!' (John 19:26–7). **l. 17 orbity:** bereavement. **l. 21 plain maps:** i.e. flat, not globes; in a sermon Donne wrote: 'In a flat map, there goes [needs] no more, to make West East . . . but to paste that flat map upon a round body, and then West and East are all one.' **l. 22 Ave, and Consummatum est:** Gabriel's first word to Mary at the Annunciation ('Hail, thou that art highly favoured': Luke 1:28), and Christ's last words on the Cross ('When Jesus therefore had received the vinegar, he said, It is finished: and he bowed his head, and gave up the ghost': John 19:30). **l. 23 court of faculties:** the authorities who administer the Church, including its festivals. **l. 24 joining these:** the Annunciation and Good Friday. **l. 25 self-fix'd pole:** the North Pole itself. **l. 26 next star:** the nearest, the Pole Star, by which sailors navigate. **l. 31 His Spirit:** the Holy Spirit. **ll. 31–2 fiery pillar . . . cloud:** God guided the Israelites through the wilderness as 'a pillar of fire' by night and as 'a pillar of a cloud' by day (Exodus 13:21). **l. 37 as God:** Christ as God. **l. 38 but one period:** the same point of time; the Creation and the Last Judgement, Donne said in a sermon, 'are not a minute asunder in respect of eternity, which hath no minutes'. **l. 39 spouse:** the Church. **l. 42 accepted:** accepted by God as sufficient. **l. 44 she all this day affords:** the Church gives us all Christ's 'pains, deeds, words' in this single day. **l. 45 gross:** the whole. **uplay:** lay up, store. **l. 46 retail:** impart in small quantities, or recount, every day.

'Good Friday, 1613. Riding Westward': Donne was riding to visit Sir Edward Herbert, elder brother of George Herbert, in Montgomery, Wales. **l. 2 intelligence:** see note to 'intelligences' in 'The Ecstasy' above.

l. 3 other spheres: the celestial ones. **l. 4 Subject to foreign motions:** in Ptolemaic astronomy the inner spheres were thought to be influenced by the ('foreign') motion of the outer. **l. 6 natural form:** natural orbit, regained in the course of the year. **l. 10 soul's form**, as opposed to bodily. **l. 11 a sun:** also, son. **by rising:** by coming into the world; by being raised on the Cross. **l. 12 by that setting:** by Christ's death. **l. 17 self life:** life itself. **must die:** cf. 'Thou canst not see my face: for there shall no man see me, and live' (Exodus 33:20). **l. 19 Nature shrink:** at the Crucifixion, 'the earth did quake, and the rocks rent' (Matthew 27:51). **l. 20 footstool:** cf. 'Thus saith the Lord, the heaven is my throne, and the earth is my footstool' (Isaiah 66:1). **the sun wink:** cf. 'the sun was darkened' (Luke 23:45). **l. 22 turn:** some versions give 'tune', 'which is perhaps right; but the chief idea here is of God's power' (Herbert J.C. Grierson, *Metaphysical Lyrics and Poems of the Seventeenth Century*, 1921). **l. 24 Zenith . . . antipodes:** highest point for us, and equally for those living on the opposite side of the globe, 'below us'. **ll. 25–6 that blood . . . The seat of all our souls:** the soul was sometimes thought to reside in the blood. **l. 26 if not of his:** whether or not Christ's soul resided in his blood. **l. 32 Half of that sacrifice:** being his mother. **l. 33 be from mine eye:** because he is looking westwards. **l. 36 the tree:** the Cross. **l. 38 Corrections:** punishments intended to correct. **leave:** leave off, cease. **l. 41 Restore thine image:** make me again in your likeness. **l. 42 turn my face:** i.e. towards you.

'To Mr Tilman after he had taken orders': Edward Tilman was ordained deacon in December 1618. **l. 3 lay-scornings:** the scorn with which some of the laity, more particularly the gentry, regarded the clerical profession. **l. 5 What bringest thou home:** what harvest have you gathered. **l. 6 vintage:** coming to maturity. **l. 8 lodestone:** magnet. **l. 10 For iron and cloth:** in exchange for iron and cloth. **l. 17 old image:** 'God created man in his own image' (Genesis 1:27). **l. 18 coronation:** ordination. **l. 24 advantage:** gain. **above, below:** show us on earth, 'below', what you have gained in heaven, 'above'. **l. 25 surmount:** exceed. **l. 27 pass:** surpass, defy. **l. 34 sublimed:** superior. **l. 36 neglect:** contempt. **l. 39 open life:** open the way to true life; perhaps, baptize. **l. 40 dignities:** titles, honours. **l. 42 convey:** communicate. **l. 46 their optics magnify:** extol their telescopes. **l. 47 brave:** fine. **engine:** instrument, means; i.e. preaching, the priestly function in general. **l. 54 hermaphrodite:** combining or concerned with opposites, heaven and earth, 'God's graces' and 'men's offences'.

'*A Hymn to Christ*': Donne travelled to Germany in May 1619 as chaplain to the Earl of Doncaster's diplomatic mission. **l. 2 Ark:** representing divine providence. **l. 9 this Island:** England. **l. 12 thy sea:** Christ's blood. **l. 17 control:** forbid. **l. 21 loving more:** loving other things than Christ. **l. 22 who ever gives, takes liberty:** i.e. Christ's gift is such that it takes away the liberty to love anyone or anything else. **l. 30 out of sight:** a long way from England; or, towards death. **l. 32 everlasting night:** death (a danger touched on in the poem's opening lines).

'*Hymn to God my God, in my Sickness*': opinion is divided as to whether Donne wrote this poem on his deathbed (as Izaak Walton stated) or during his serious illness in the winter of 1623. **l. 1 holy room:** heaven. **l. 4 instrument:** possibly, the poetic faculty. **l. 6 their love:** their loving care of him. **l. 9 south-west discovery:** through the Strait of Magellan; here, 'south' suggests heat and 'west' (the setting of the sun) death, i.e. death by fever. **l. 10 *Per fretum febris*:** through the strait (also, the raging heat) of fever. **l. 11 straits:** also in the sense of 'sufferings'. **l. 13 my west:** my death (where the sun sets). **east:** where the sun rises, hence the Resurrection. **ll. 16–17 Pacific Sea . . . eastern riches:** signifying the peace and joys of heaven. **l. 18 Anyan:** or Anian Strait, presumed north-west passage (sometimes identified with the Bering Strait) from the Atlantic Ocean to the Pacific. **l. 20 Japhet . . . Cham . . . Shem:** sons of Noah; Japhet populated Europe, Cham (Ham) Africa, and Shem Asia. **ll. 21–2 Paradise and Calvary . . . stood in one place:** a traditional belief. **l. 22 tree:** the Tree of Knowledge, bearing the forbidden fruit. **l. 23 both Adams:** Adam and Christ. **l. 24 the first Adam's sweat:** cf. 'In the sweat of thy face shalt thou eat bread' (Genesis 3:19); here, the sweat of fever. **l. 26 purple:** redeeming blood; also, royal cloak. **l. 27 his thorns:** the poet's own sufferings. **l. 30 Therefore that:** in order that.

'*A Hymn to God the Father*': 'The poem's refrains are informed by two puns personal to Donne, the obvious one on his name (Donne/done), and the less obvious one on the maiden name of his wife Ann (More/more)' (C.A. Patrides, *John Donne: The Complete English Poems*, 1985). **l. 1 that sin where I begun:** original sin, in which he was born. **l. 14 perish on the shore:** i.e. perish eternally. **l. 15 thy son:** also, sun.